Word, Care, and Worship

GLOBAL LIBRARY

In this second volume of his biblical theology series, Professor Nyende has provided a much-needed synthesis of shepherd leadership, a vital concept across the canon. Nyende recognizes the role of prophets and priests as Old Testament prototypes for New Testament preachers and teachers, who extend the ministry of Jesus, the chief shepherd of the church. Nyende is both scholar and pastor as he unpacks the practical implications for contemporary church leadership. I believe that this work contributes to a movement directed by the Holy Spirit to frame pastoral ministry in terms of spiritual shepherding. It is a return to biblical precedents needed in every corner of the world.

Timothy S. Laniak, ThD
Senior Professor of Biblical Studies,
Gordon-Conwell Theological Seminary, Massachusetts, USA
Senior Vice President of Global Content,
Our Daily Bread Ministries

Peter Nyende thoughtfully compiles the biblical evidence for three key areas of church ministry, centred around the image of Jesus as the chief shepherd of God's flock. Students of Jesus and of ministry will benefit from engaging with these topics – especially Nyende's forceful demonstration that scriptural teaching about the kingdom of God was central to Jesus's mission and remains central to those seeking to shepherd his church today.

Andrew Malone
Lecturer in Biblical Studies,
Ridley College, Melbourne, Australia

In *Word, Care, and Worship*, Professor Nyende addresses a missing dimension in the literature on pastoral theology. While much of the literature focusses on the techniques of pastoral care, this book focusses on the foundation of all pastoral ministry in a thorough treatment of the biblical witness on the tasks of shepherding. The information in this work is indispensable for everyone who ventures into pastoral ministry.

James W. Thompson, PhD
Scholar in Residence, Graduate School of Theology,
Abilene Christian University, Texas, USA

Having already established himself as an African biblical scholar who takes seriously the church's need to understand the full scope of the biblical story (see his book *The Restoration of God's Dwelling and Kingdom: A Biblical Theology*), Peter Nyende now provides a much-needed follow-up volume in his new book, *Word, Care, and Worship*. Writing with pastors and pastors-in-training in mind, Nyende's new study is both practical and biblical. Not willing to leave the Bible as a specimen of the ancient past (as some scholars do) or simply hand out advice untested by Scripture (as some popular writers do), Nyende gives the reader a biblical theology that is truly in service to the church. Beginning with the Bible's dominant image of the pastor as shepherd, Nyende situates teaching and preaching as the pastor's primary work, while not neglecting the crucial tasks of pastoral care of those in need and the facilitation of worship. Nyende has provided a careful, readable text that will be useful for pastors and theological students throughout Africa – and globally!

Grant LeMarquand, ThD
Emeritus Professor of Biblical Studies,
Trinity Anglican Seminary, Pennsylvania, USA
Retired Anglican Bishop for the Horn of Africa

Word, Care, and Worship

A Biblical Theology of Pastoral Ministry

Peter Nyende

© 2025 Peter Nyende

Published 2025 by Langham Global Library
An imprint of Langham Publishing
www.langhampublishing.org

Langham Publishing and its imprints are a ministry of Langham Partnership

Langham Partnership
PO Box 296, Carlisle, Cumbria, CA3 9WZ, UK
www.langham.org

ISBNs:
978-1-78641-057-3 Print
978-1-78641-159-4 ePub
978-1-78641-160-0 PDF

Peter Nyende has asserted his right under the Copyright, Designs and Patents Act, 1988 to be identified as the Author of this work.

All rights reserved. No part of this publication may be reproduced, stored in a retrieval system or transmitted, in any form or by any means, electronic, mechanical, photocopying, recording or otherwise, without the prior written permission of the publisher or the Copyright Licensing Agency.

Requests to reuse content from Langham Publishing are processed through PLSclear. Please visit www.plsclear.com to complete your request.

Unless otherwise stated, Scripture quotations are taken from the New Revised Standard Version Bible, copyright © 1989 National Council of the Churches of Christ in the United States of America. Used by permission. All rights reserved.

Scripture quotations marked (ESV) are taken from The Holy Bible, English Standard Version®(ESV®), copyright © 2001 by Crossway, a publishing ministry of Good News Publishers. Used by permission. All rights reserved.

Scripture quotations marked (NIV) are taken from the Holy Bible, New International Version®, NIV®. Copyright © 1973, 1978, 1984, 2011 by Biblica, Inc.™ Used by permission of Zondervan.

Scripture quotations marked (RSV) are taken from Revised Standard Version of the Bible, copyright © 1946, 1952, and 1971 National Council of the Churches of Christ in the United States of America. Used by permission. All rights reserved.

Scripture quotations marked (GNB) are from the Good News Translation in Today's English Version – Second Edition Copyright © 1992 by American Bible Society. Used by Permission.

Scripture quotations marked (NEB) are taken from the New English Bible, copyright © Cambridge University Press and Oxford University Press 1961, 1970. All rights reserved.

British Library Cataloguing-in-Publication Data
A catalogue record for this book is available from the British Library

ISBN: 978-1-78641-057-3

Cover & Book Design: projectluz.com

Langham Partnership actively supports theological dialogue and an author's right to publish but does not necessarily endorse the views and opinions set forth here or in works referenced within this publication, nor can we guarantee technical and grammatical correctness. Langham Partnership does not accept any responsibility or liability to persons or property as a consequence of the reading, use or interpretation of its published content.

To Josephine Njoki Naliaka, my delightful constant companion in life

Contents

Preface xi
Abbreviations xiii
1 Introduction 1
2 Shepherds and Sheep in the Old Testament 13
3 Preaching and Teaching the Word: the Primary Activities in Pastoral Ministry 35
4 Care for Those in Difficulties: An Integral Part of Pastoral Ministry ... 71
5 Facilitating Worship: The Priestly Task of Pastoral Ministry 93
6 Practical Recommendations for Primary Activities in Pastoral Ministry 117
Bibliography 125
Index 131

Preface

This book is the second in my four-volume study on biblical theology, all of which has been inspired by nearly a quarter of a century of class interactions with my theology students in Africa. These interactions have allowed me to see more clearly the interests and pressing concerns of churches in Africa, as well as grasp well their unique challenges and pitfalls. However, given that the studies are based on the contents of the Bible, the volumes will invariably be of interest to theological students and scholars from any location or background. I have not tailored them for an exclusively African audience.

This volume itself was brought about by a disturbing observation I have made for years in my interaction with different sets of students. On the one hand, students exhibit little, or sketchy, scriptural knowledge for pastoral ministry, yet that is the essence of the training in which they have enrolled. On the other hand, there are very few books I can turn to as resources for my teaching on pastoral ministry which look at the practice from a biblical prism. This state of affairs drove me to begin my own scriptural studies on pastoral ministry. Initially, starting in 2016, I shared my studies with my students whose placements (or practical training in pastoral ministry) I was responsible for, and with pastors through retreats and seminars. Eventually, I dedicated time to develop my studies into an in-depth one, which resulted in this book.

As with the first volume in this series,[1] my approach in writing this book mirrors my theology classes in Africa in the following ways. In order to foster a direct, personal grasp and knowledge of the Bible, I have ensured that it is the primary subject of the study. Bible references, textual quotes, and their study are therefore considerably more numerous than references from scholarly books on the Bible's content. That said, as a Bible scholar myself, I do not neglect biblical scholarship nor extra-biblical sources in my study, though in this work I only engage them when I find them to be vital in my exegesis of a given Bible text. I hope that my readers, particularly seasoned Bible scholars, will appreciate this spirit of my study as well as its alluded merits.

Special thanks to Dr. Nigel Rooms, the coordinator of partnership for Missional Church UK and co-editor of the journal *Ecclesial Futures,* for the time

---

1. Peter Nyende, *The Restoration of God's Dwelling and Kingdom: A Biblical Theology* (Carlisle: Langham Global Library, 2023).

he took to read through all the first-draft chapters of this book and point out what was unclear or confusing, and suggest improvements where he could. Thanks also to Dr. Chris Howles, the director of cross-cultural training at Oak Hill College, London (with whom I closely worked with when he was teaching at Namugongo Martyrs Seminary in Kampala, Uganda), for allowing me to use him as a sounding board to my discussions on every chapter of this book. Their generosity has made the book clearer than it would otherwise have been.

I cannot forget the debt I continually owe my lovely spouse, Josephine, to whom I have dedicated this book. Uninterrupted time in solitude is indispensable to my writing; her forbearing companionship afforded it to me in large measure and much more besides.

As with the first volume, I would like to thank the One in whom "we live, breath, and have our being" for enabling me to write this second volume on matters I deem important to kingdom business. He knows the end from the beginning and everything has a time in line with his plans and purposes. To him be reserved always the ultimate glory and honour for our efforts whose fruits see the light of day.

Abbreviations

AB	The Anchor Bible
Bib	*Biblica*
Bsac	*Bibliotheca Sacra*
CBQ	*Catholic Biblical Quarterly*
Colloq	*Colloquium*
ESV	The English Standard Bible
ESBT	Essential Studies in Biblical Theology
GNB	Good News Bible
Hermeneia	Hermeneia, New International Bible Commentary
HTR	*Harvard Theological Review*
IJPT	*International Journal of Practical Theology*
IVPNTC	IVP New Testament Commentary Series
JORH	*Journal of Religion and Health*
JAOS	*Journal of the American Oriental Society*
JBL	*Journal of Biblical Literature*
JSNTSup	Journal for the Society of the New Testament: Supplementary Series
JSOTSup	Journal of the Study of the Old Testament Supplementary Series
LXX	Septuagint
Neot	*Neotestamentica*
NIGTC	New International Greek Testament Commentary
NSBT	New Studies in Biblical Theology
NEB	New English Bible
NICNT	New International Commentary on the New Testament
NICOT	New International Commentary on the Old Testament
NIV	New International Version
NRSV	New Revised Standard Version
NSBT	New Studies in Biblical Theology
NTS	*New Testament Studies*
NovT	*Novum Testamentum*
Proc	*Proceedings*
RSV	Revised Standard Bible
SSBT	Short Studies in Biblical Theology

SNTSMS	Society for New Testament Studies Monograph Series
Them	*Themelios*
TS	*Theological Studies*
ThTo	*Theology Today*
ResQ	*Restoration Quarterly*
VT	*Vetus Testamentum*
VigChr	*Vigiliae Christinae*
WBC	Word Biblical Commentary
b. Pesaḥ	*Pesahim*

1

Introduction

1. Liturgies and Pastoral Ministry

Usually the work of pastors is understood in the context of the churches they run, the persons in the congregations or parishes they are responsible for, and the services they offer. But this does not mean that the work of pastors is entirely clear. For this reason, I have wondered which resources or literature would be available to those training to be pastors (referred to from here on as "ordinands" following how they are called in Anglican theological colleges) to help them understand the pastoral ministry for which they are preparing.

The first readily available literature that ordinands could turn to are liturgies of ordination. These liturgies are prepared for the ordination of pastors. They are meant to enlighten the ordinands regarding their work, and lead in prayers for God to energize them by his Spirit. Liturgies of ordination therefore mention and give some detail of the work expected of pastors. They may also have Bible readings related to pastoral ministry.

A case in point are the liturgies of ordination of the Anglican church to which I belong. In the 1662 *Book of Common Prayer*'s ordination charge for priests (which was the liturgy used at my ordination), the designate priests are told that they are to teach, premonish, feed the flock under their care, and to seek the lost sheep. They are told that they are shepherds of the sheep of Christ, messengers, watchmen, and stewards of the Lord. The following three Scriptures are read out in the service: Ephesians 4:7–13, Matthew 9:36–38, and John 10:1–16. Matthew 9:36–38 contains Jesus's instructions to pray for shepherds in view of the many sheep who lack one. John 10:1–16 is Jesus's self-disclosure as the good shepherd and what such a shepherd does, while Ephesians reveals that the building up of believers is the ultimate reason God has made some to be, amongst others, pastors who are also teachers. In addition, the ordinands are given authority to preach God's word as a Bible is given to them. They are also given authority to celebrate the sacraments in all the places they will be appointed to serve.

Going by the example of the Anglican liturgy of ordination, liturgies of ordination, in principle, point in the right direction concerning the work of a pastor. They do so because they mention the various roles of a pastor, and give some Scripture readings on pastoral ministry. However, ordinands relying on a liturgy of ordination to understand their pastoral ministry will receive little guidance on how and why, for example, they are to teach, be a watchman or messenger. So, whereas liturgies of ordination give areas of pastoral ministry, they do not explain the know-how, nor discuss the reasons for and the ends, of those areas of pastoral ministry.

2. Pastoral Ministry Handbooks and Pastoral Ministry

Ordinands have handbooks or manuals to turn to for an understanding of pastoral ministry. Like all handbooks, pastoral ministry handbooks are guidebooks and as such discuss concretely pastoral ministry activities and are straightforward on how those activities are executed. These are very handy and helpful to ordinands in helping them learn how to go about executing various pastoral ministry activites. So, for example, Croft's handbook covers the following activities: guarding the truth, preaching the word, praying for the flock, setting an example, visiting the sick, comforting the grieving, caring for widows, confronting sin, encouraging the weak, and training leaders.[1] Hughes's handbook discusses the following: Sunday worship, annual services, weddings, funerals, public prayers, creeds, hymns and songs, baptisms, communion, pastoral counselling, and hospital visits.[2]

Taken together, the handbooks of Croft and Hughes cover eighteen areas of pastoral ministry. That list of pastoral ministry areas covered in pastoral ministry handbooks would be longer if we included more examples of such books. This abundance is bewildering, leaving ordinands with no clear sense of what the core pastoral functions are that they need to know how to execute. I suspect that this is the reason why, roughly sixty years ago, Johnson complained that pastors were being torn apart by the demands on them, resulting

---

1. Brian Croft, *The Pastor's Ministry: Biblical Priorities for Faithful Shepherds* (Grand Rapids: Zondervan, 2015).

2. R. Kent Hughes, *The Pastor's Book: A Comprehensive and Practical Guide to Pastoral Ministry* (Wheaton: Crossway, 2015).

in his call for a redefinition of pastoral ministry.[3] In his words, "[t]he vocation of a pastor needs to be defined more clearly, for in our time it is loaded with complexities and conflicting expectations."[4] The situation had not changed thirty years after Johnson's call, as seen in the sweeping remarks of John Stott: "One feature of the contemporary church is its uncertainty about the role of its professional ministers. Are they primarily social workers, psychiatrists, educators, facilitators, administrators, or what?"[5]

We should also note that pastoral ministry manuals do not discuss the undercurrents of pastoral ministry – such as their bases and nature – nor do they discuss the goals of the pastoral ministry activities on which they give guidance. This is because handbooks do not set out specifically to address the factors behind pastoral ministry nor its goals. Yet such knowledge is vital if pastoral ministry is not to be carried out mechanically (simply as the execution of a set of roles or tasks in a prescribed way). Knowing what informs the activities of pastoral ministry and their ends means that pastors conducting them would have a sense of both their transcendent nature and divine goals.

3. Pastoral Theology Literature and Pastoral Ministry

The last literature ordinands could turn to for an understanding of pastoral ministry is pastoral theology literature. In it one can acquire knowledge of the bases, nature, and intentions of pastoral ministry, which in other words is the comprehensive knowledge of pastoral ministry which we have alluded to. Such comprehensive understanding of pastoral ministry covers its foundations, core activities, the content or details of those activities, its goals, and the requisite qualities (the character and mentality) of a pastor. Moreover, pastoral theology literature engages critically with pastoral ministry with respect to its history, its parameters, prospects, and future possibilities, and it also covers practical ecclesial studies.

However, a look at current and relatively recent pastoral theology literature shows that it is far removed from pastoral ministry and is too complex to be of help to ordinands seeking to understand pastoral ministry. Pastoral theology literature would therefore fall short of providing ordinands with the much-needed comprehensive knowledge of pastoral ministry.

---

3. Paul E. Johnson, "A Theology of Pastoral Care," JORH 3, no. 2 (1964): 171–175.
4. Johnson, "A Theology of Pastoral Care," 171.
5. John R. W. Stott, "Ideals of Pastoral Ministry," *Bsac* 146, no. 581 (1989): 3–11.

Comprehensive knowledge of pastoral ministry may have been possible to attain for earlier generations of ordinands when pastoral theology literature addressed pastoral work and churches as its context. Historians of pastoral theology point out that up to the 1960s the prevailing paradigm in pastoral theology studies was "clerical" and/or "ecclesial."[6] However, from the 1970s onwards pastoral theology literature moved beyond pastors and churches to society and its various institutions, and beyond persons in churches to clients and other potential beneficiaries of pastoral work. Pastoral theology literature expanded to address living faiths alongside Christianity. Accordingly pastoral theology literature looked into, and addressed, audiences beyond pastors and church members they served. Although some pastoral theology literature was concerned with pastors and churches, and with clinical pastoral ministry (pastoral counselling informed by psychotherapeutic theories and practices), the focus of the literature was on a very broad range of Christian and other religious practices in the contexts within which they existed. And although there were biblical and theological reflections on Christian practices, they were mainly reflected upon, and investigated, by insights from the discipline of social sciences.

I remember my student days in the late 1990s when I was a Masters student of pastoral theology struggling to no avail to relate pastoral theology to pastoral ministry. This state of affairs troubled me. After all, I was undertaking my Masters studies due to my commitments, by means of wider knowledge on the subject, to offer leadership in pastoral ministry in my church. Most of the literature I read was, in subject matter, not concerned specifically with pastors nor their congregations or parishes, but with wider audiences. Graham's and Lartey's books suffice as good examples here. Graham's book was about feminism; essentially a sustained critique of androcentrism in the Bible and society and not about pastoral ministry in the context of pastors and churches.[7] Lartey's book was meant to be about cultural and religious pluralism as the context of pastoral care and counselling.[8] The way he addressed pastoral care and counselling was odd to me. He removed the understanding of pastoral care

---

6. See Roest for a comprehensive summary on pastoral theology studies: Henk de Roest, *Collaborative Practical Theology: Engaging Practitioners in Research on Christian Practices* (Leiden: Brill, 2020), 90–130.

7. Elaine L. Graham, *Transforming Practise: Pastoral Theology in an Age of Uncertainty* (London: Mowbray, 1996).

8. Emmanuel Y. Lartey, *In Living Colour: An Intercultural Approach to Pastoral Care and Counselling* (London: SPCK, 1997). There is a second edition of the book published in 2003 by Jessica Kingsley Publishers.

from what a pastor does to generally mean empowering, nurturing, reconciling, guiding, healing, and sustaining. He also shifted the context of pastoral care and counselling from pastors and churches to an indefinite location of representative persons, care givers, small groups, faith communities, and even nations etc.

This form of pastoral theology literature has endured into the twenty-first century and is demonstrated in the available pastoral literature in Africa which is the context within which I work. As pointed out in Magezi's study, pastoral theology literature in Africa – which come in the names of African theology, Black theology, reconstruction theology etc. – engages chiefly with the lived experiences, beliefs, and realities of African peoples via theological reflection and for theological ends.[9] In other words, pastoral theology literature in Africa is not particularly concerned with pastoral ministry in African churches. It is instructive that Magezi does not mention, in his proposals for the task of practical theology in Africa, the study of the ministry of pastors in African churches. To him the task of practical theology in Africa is to deal with the unique challenges of Africa's heterogeneity, to develop "a framework that includes practical spirituality, social, physical, political and economic issues,"[10] and to reflect theologically on the numerous churches that continue to spring up all over Africa.

This lack of a particular concern for pastoral ministry in pastoral theology literature from Africa is also demonstrated in an anthology from African scholars on pastoral theology, *Pastoral Care in African Christianity: Challenging Essays in Pastoral Theology*.[11] Apart from healing,[12] pastoral care of clergy,[13] and their problems,[14] none of the eleven essays in this volume addresses pastors and their congregations and parishes as the subject of pastoral ministry in Africa. In other words, the subject of these studies is not concerned with pastors (what they need, or need to know, or what they do or need to do, or what skills they

---

9. Vhumani Magezi, "Practical Theology in Africa: Situation, Approaches, Framework and Agenda Proposition," *IJPT* 23, no. 1 (2019): 115–135.

10. Magezi, "Practical Theology in Africa," 133.

11. Douglas W. Waruta and Hannah W. Kinoti, eds., *Pastoral Care in African Christianity: Challenging Essays in Pastoral Theology*, 2nd ed. (Nairobi: Acton Publishers, 2000).

12. Philomena N. Mwaura, "Healing as a Pastoral Concern," in Waruta and Kinoti, *Pastoral Care*, 72–97.

13. Laurenti Magezi, "Pastoral Care of Clergy," in Waruta and Kinoti, *Pastoral Care*, 219–242.

14. C. M. Mwikambi, "Challenges and Problems of the Clergy," in Waruta and Kinoti, *Pastoral Care*, 243–266.

need peculiar to churches in Africa), nor is it concerned with congregations or parishes (their needs, nurture, modes and styles, care, disciplining of beliefs and thinking, inculcating required behavioural codes etc.). Like typical pastoral theology books, their subjects are students, youth, marriage, violence, ageing, street children etc., while the context of their discussion is well beyond pastors and their congregations.

For the reasons alluded to above, pastoral theology from the 1980s became practical theology with pastoral theology designated as one of its branches. As a branch of practical theology, pastoral theology addressed pastoral ministry in the classical sense but never comprehensively. By this I mean that (with the exception of pastoral ministry handbooks and a few pastoral theology books)[15] pastoral theology literature dealt only with an aspect of pastoral ministry divorced from the whole edifice of pastors and churches, their work, and the contexts they inhabit. They thus lacked an overarching framework within which to give perspective to the discussed pastoral ministry. This state of pastoral theology literature is also demonstrated in Africa by pastoral theology books from Africa.[16]

Ordinands turning to pastoral theology literature would therefore stand little chance of encountering work that would offer them a comprehensive understanding of pastoral ministry. Whether they turn to the liturgy, or to handbooks of pastoral ministry, or to pastoral theology literature, or to some combination of the three they are likely to fall short of having the comprehensive knowledge of pastoral ministry they so desire.

4. Effects of Limited Understandings of Pastoral Ministry

Ordinands with scanty knowledge of pastoral ministry are undesirable on two accounts. The first is that pastors are likely to fail to appreciate the ministry's core activities and goals. This lack of appreciation will result in pastors' inability to focus their energies deliberately on the essential activities of the ministry with their intended outcomes in mind. Not knowing exactly what is essential

---

15. See Thomas Oden, *Pastoral Theology* (San Francisco: Harper and Row, 1983); William H. Willimon, *Pastor: A Reader for Ordained Ministry* (Nashville: Abingdon Press, 2002); David Hoyle, *The Pattern of our Calling: Ministry Yesterday, Today and Tomorrow* (London: SCM Press, 2016); and Daniel L. Akin, *Pastoral Theology: Theological Foundations for Who a Pastor is and What he Does* (Nashville: B&H Academic, 2017).

16. Daisy Nwachuku and Jean Masamba ma Mpolo, eds., *Pastoral Care and Counselling in Africa Today*, African Pastoral Studies Vol. 1 (Bern: Peter Lang, 1991); and Abraham Adu Berinyuu, *Towards Theory and Practice of Pastoral Counseling in Africa* (Bern: Peter Lang, 1990).

in pastoral ministry, and the reasons why, will also lead to their failure to invest in acquiring the required competencies to execute its most significant activities. In such a scenario, God's people in congregations and parishes are in danger of being bereft of essential pastoral services, and/or are at the mercy of ill-equipped pastors.

Second, since human actions are not mechanical but fuelled by motivation, imprecise knowledge on the origins, essential activities and objectives of pastoral ministry results in pastors whose motivations are likely not derived from God's commands, purposes, and goals, thus lacking in transcendent and ethical dimensions. They could, for example, be motivated largely by what they simply need. Such needs could include any, or a combination, of the following: money, livelihood, prestige, power, recognition, and fame. Pastoral work is then undertaken fundamentally to meet their egoistic needs. Others may be motivated largely by the desire to please their superiors. In such cases, their pastoral ministry is structured around what receives the approval of their superiors. Some could be motivated largely by the desire to please their parishioners and thus concentrate on pastoral activities that please them. Still others may be motivated largely by competition; the drive to perform better than others in pastoral ministry. In my experience it is not uncommon to have pastors confess to wanting to have more people in their churches than some other churches or religious groups, to have more outreaches than others, preaching to more people, raising more money, having better facilities, being more visible, more charismatic, more liturgical etc. than others.

Inability to relate pastoral ministry to God and derive their motivation thereby means that pastors may lack the perseverance needed in ministry, or they may find the responsibility of pastoral ministry intolerable. Difficult times will arise for pastors and have been known to be caused, for example, by aggravating congregants, rejection, sabotage, hostile superiors, lack of support, lack of progress in ministry, lack of recognition, persecution, and harsh socio-economic environments. A lack of spiritual motivation may also lead pastors to ignore the ethical dimension integral to their conduct of pastoral ministry. Where pastors vacate pastoral ministry for lack of perseverance, God's people stand in danger of being abandoned by pastors and denied pastoral services altogether. Where pastors are not constrained but unhindered ethically in their conduct of pastoral ministry, churches are most likely to suffer conflicts, financial exploitation, psychological manipulation and bullying, emotional abuse, deceit etc. from wayward pastors. There are churches here in my African context that have been known even to disintegrate under unethical pastors.

5. Necessity of the Bible for a Comprehensive Knowledge of Pastoral Theology

As can be gathered, I have inquired into literature on pastoral ministry from the perspective of the needs of ordinands because it is with their needs in mind that I have undertaken this study (although I also have in mind pastors who for various reasons wish to reflect more deeply on pastoral ministry). With ordinands in mind, I have demonstrated the significance of, and therefore need for, pastoral theology literature that provides comprehensive knowledge of pastoral ministry because it examines the fundamental activities of pastors, and the transcendent nature of pastoral ministry, and discusses its goals. To me the availability of such literature to ordinands is imperative given that theological literature is critical to their learning and teaching in theological colleges, seminaries, schools of divinity, and university departments of theology.

It is absolutely necessary that biblical studies scholarship on pastoral ministry contributes to making such pastoral theology literature available (for which reason that I have written this book). Pastoral theology that draws directly from the Scriptures is of first importance to understanding pastoral ministry since the Bible, as the supreme locale of God's communication, should be privileged in informing the faith, life, worldview, and, crucially for our study, the work and identity of pastors. Consequently, the Bible must foremost, above all other sources of revelation and theology, be brought to bear on ordinands' and pastors' understanding of pastoral ministry. Biblical studies literature on pastoral ministry is therefore fundamental to, and should be part and parcel of, the needed pastoral theology literature.

We should note that we already have some biblical studies literature which enlightens its readers on some aspects of pastoral ministry such as pastoral activities, the foundations and goals of pastoral ministry, and pastoral care. We have one Bible study book that looks at pastoral ministry from the perspective of the Gospels and the letters of Paul,[17] one that looks at pastoral ministry as enlightened by the Epistles of Paul,[18] and one that looks at Paul's pastoral care in 1 Thessalonians from the perspective of Greek moral philosophers.[19] There are eight chapters of Bible studies on pastoral ministry in a book volume on *Paul*

---

17. Jonathan F. Grothe, *Reclaiming Patterns of Pastoral Ministry: Jesus and Paul* (St. Louise: Concordia, 1988).

18. James W. Thompson, *Pastoral Ministry According to Paul: A Biblical Vision* (Grand Rapids: Eerdmans, 2006).

19. Abraham J. Malherbe, *Paul and the Thessalonians: The Philosophic Tradition of Pastoral Care* (Eugene: Wipf and Stock, 2011).

as Pastor[20] with each chapter's understanding of pastoral ministry enlightened respectively by Acts, Romans, 1 Corinthians, Galatians, Ephesians, Philippians, Colossians, and 1 Thessalonians. Last, there are seven journal articles drawing from the New Testament,[21] Gospels,[22] Matthew,[23] Acts 21,[24] Pauline Epistles,[25] the Pastoral Epistles,[26] and 1 Thessalonians respectively[27] for an understanding of pastoral ministry.

But more needs to be done if Bible studies are to contribute to pastoral theology literature that fosters comprehensive knowledge of pastoral ministry. In particular, Bible studies on pastoral ministry that look at the whole Bible on pastoral ministry are required because, by drawing from the whole Bible, they would inevitably give us a more comprehensive picture of pastoral ministry from the Scriptures.

Unfortunately, such studies on pastoral ministry do not exist. Laniak's work[28] comes closest to undertaking such a study: it looks at the whole Bible in relationship to leadership when it is viewed metaphorically as shepherding. Although Laniak's study is not strictly speaking a Bible study on pastoral ministry (which is the reason I did not include it in the list of biblical studies literature above), it has the potential to teach from the whole Bible about pastoral ministry as one type of Christian leadership. This is what Laniak ventured to do in his concluding chapters by focussing on the implications of his biblical theology of leadership for pastoral ministry.[29] In this book, I build on what Laniak has done in his Bible study, by conducting an exclusive examination of pastoral ministry in the whole Bible. In other words, this book

---

20. Brians S. Rosner, Andrew S. Malone, and Trevor J. Burke, eds., *Paul as Pastor* (London: T&T Clark, 2018).

21. S. Maclean Gilmour, "'Pastoral Care' in the New Testament Church," *NTS* 10 (1964): 393–398.

22. W. C. Mavis, "Jesus's Influence on the Pastoral Ministry," *Theology Today* 4, no. 3 (1947): 357–367.

23. Carson E. Reed, "Practical Theology in Diverse Ethnic Community: Matthew's Gospel as a Model of Ministry," *ResQ* 60.3 (2018): 163–170.

24. John R. W. Stott, "Ideals of Pastoral Ministry," *Bsac* 146.581 (1989): 3–11.

25. William R. Edwards, "Participants in What We Proclaim: Recovering Paul's Narrative of Pastoral Ministry," *Them* 39.3 (2014): 455–469.

26. Joseph A. Fitzmyer, "The Structured Ministry of the Church in the Pastoral Epistles," *CBQ* 66.4 (2004): 582–596.

27. Abraham J. Malherbe, "'Pastoral Care' in the Thessalonian Church," *NTS* 36 (1990): 375–391.

28. Timothy S. Laniak, *Shepherds After My Own Heart: Pastoral Traditions and Leadership in the Bible*, NSBT 20 (Downers Grove: InterVarsity Press, 2006).

29. Laniak, *Shepherds After My Own Heart*, 247–253.

is a biblical theology of pastoral ministry. I hope that this biblical theology will help ordinands understand comprehensively pastoral ministry from a biblical perspective.

6. The Book's Approach and Design

Within the context of instructions to pastors (referred to as "elders" – *presbuteroi*), Jesus was referred to in the first Epistle of Peter as the chief shepherd (*tou archipoimenos*):

> Now, as an elder myself . . . I exhort the elders among you to tend the flock of God that is in your charge, exercising the oversight, not under compulsion but willingly, as God would have you do it . . . Do not lord it over those in your charge, but be examples to the flock. And when the chief shepherd appears, you will win the crown of glory that never fades. (1 Pet 5:1–5)[30]

On the basis of this revelation from 1 Peter, I have approached my study of the whole Bible's content on pastoral ministry by centring on Jesus; what we can learn about the ministry from Jesus himself in the Gospels. Understanding pastoral ministry from Jesus as presented in the Gospels has invariably led me to discuss the Old Testament whose literature casts into sharper relief Jesus's pastoral ministry as portrayed in the Gospels.

However, Jesus's pastoral ministry did not end with his physical departure from the world. He shared his ministry with the Twelve by commissioning them to continue his work. This commissioning is particularly represented in the commissioning of Peter by Jesus to feed and take care of his flock (John 21:15–18) which is a commissioning he received on behalf of the Twelve. Thus, in my approach to examining the whole Bible on pastoral ministry, I have subsequently looked at the operations and teachings of the apostles in the rest of the writings of the New Testament. I have used my study of apostolic operations and teachings to demonstrate, elaborate, and clarify the teachings on pastoral ministry which I have derived from the content of Jesus's pastoral ministry in the Gospels.

As a whole Bible study on pastoral ministry, my methodology places the Bible in the foreground of the study, and thus truly fosters a biblical understanding of pastoral ministry. For this reason, the Bible itself and not schol-

---

30. Bible quotes are from the New Revised Standard Version; I indicate when a quotation is not from the NRSV.

arly literature is the primary content of discussion in this study. I have kept pastoral theology literature, and views of Bible scholars, at a minimum by limiting their references and/or use to where they are crucial in enlightening the Bible passage under discussion. This approach accounts for the numerous exegeses of Bible passages (and their references and quotations) in the book's discussion and fewer references to scholarly literature on those Bible passages. Furthermore, to keep the Bible itself at the centre of this whole Bible study on pastoral ministry, the context which I have given priority in my exegesis is the Bible itself – the Bible content that precedes and succeeds relevant texts under study. It is only in instances where the context of the Bible does not shed light on a text that I have sought extra-biblical sources for a context to help enlighten a text.

From the pastoral ministry of Jesus, which is rooted in the shepherding responsibilities of priests and prophets in the Old Testament, I have isolated three key areas of pastoral ministry: "preaching and teaching the word of God," "caring for those in difficulties," and "facilitating worship." I have accordingly structured my whole Bible study on pastoral ministry around these three key areas whereby I discuss preaching to, and teaching, God's people in Chapter 3, caring for God's people who are in difficulties in Chapter 4, and leading the gathered in approaching God in Chapter 5.

However, I precede this whole Bible study by a discussion in Chapter 2 on the meaning of shepherd/pastor (*poimēn*). On the basis of the meaning and metaphorical use of *poimēn* in the Old Testament, I argue that Jesus's identity and operations as revealed in the Gospels can be viewed from a kingship perspective, of Jesus as the promised Davidic king. This is the fundamental and executive understanding of Jesus as *poimēn* because it directly relates Jesus's person and work in the Old Testament as a continuation of the story, and thus the fulfilment of God's promise that the promised Davidic king would be a good shepherd (*poimēn*). But I shall also argue on the basis of 1 Peter 5:1–5 (and related Scriptures) that Jesus's identity and operations as a pastor (*poimēn*) can also be viewed from a non-executive shepherding responsibility, captured in the role of priests and prophets in the Old Testament which Jesus executed. The fundamental kingship understanding of Jesus as *poimēn* we have just pointed out does not therefore nullify this pastoral understanding of the same, nor does it make it of less significance. This viewpoint of Jesus as pastor is the foundation upon which my whole Bible study on pastoral ministry is built.

2

Shepherds and Sheep in the Old Testament

Pastor is a word directly taken from the Latin for shepherd. Therefore, to call ordained clergy or ministers shepherds instead of pastors is actually legitimate, for the two are synonymous. Not only is it in harmony with Jesus's own self reference (John 10:11), but also the way followers of Jesus who led others were referred to (1 Pet 5:1–5). However, the understanding of Jesus as a pastor is not to be sought from its Latin context because his pastoral responsibilities stemmed directly from the Old Testament's metaphorical use of shepherd, and thus Israel's shepherds. We must pay attention to this context and usage to appreciate fully the New Testament's revelation of Jesus as a pastor. We will begin our study by examining the meaning of the term "shepherd" in the Old Testament and consequently how it was used metaphorically. Understanding the metaphorical use of shepherds-sheep in the Old Testament will open the way for us to look at shepherds in the Old Testament; their identity and what they did, or were supposed to do, for the people. This discussion will lay the foundation for our understanding of Jesus as a shepherd and thereby help us to study his pastoral ministry (and that of his disciples) in succeeding chapters.

1. "Shepherd" and "To Shepherd" in the Old Testament

In Old Testament Hebrew, the term for shepherd is *ra'ah* (while in the Old Testament's Greek translation, it is *poimēn*). As a verb, "to shepherd" has a variety of meanings in the Old Testament. It could mean to lead to pasture, graze, or feed (e.g. Gen 41:2; Exod 34:3; Isa 5:17). It, and other words related to the same concept, could also mean to tend or care for (e.g. 2 Sam 7:8; Ps 95:7; Ezek 34:15). It could further still mean leading (Exod 3:1; 1 Chr 11:2;

and Isa 40:11). Finally, the terms could also mean to own sheep (Exod 3:1; 1 Sam 25:16; Amos 7:14); for which reason, the term *ra'ah* could also mean a "keeper of sheep" (Gen 4:2). Thus, the term shepherd in the Old Testament was a label for people who took care of sheep. This caring for flocks was so intertwined with shepherds that their work was communicated using that verb: to shepherd. In other words, if we translated this sense through the use of crude English, "shepherds shepherded."

The concepts of shepherds and shepherding in the Old Testament were defined by their literal pastoral context. The Israelites were a semi-pastoral people who relied significantly on their flocks for meat, milk and fat, clothing, trumpets, oil flasks etc. But their sheep could not take care of themselves. They needed people to lead them all (including pregnant ewes and little lambs) to pastures for grazing, to water for drinking, and to places where they could lie down to chew their cud and rest, as well as sleep at night. They also needed people to keep them together, to protect them from perilous weather, predators and thieves, to rescue them from traps and places they could not get out of, search for them when they strayed, and nurse them when they were injured or weak. Those who undertook all these pastoral responsibilities were labelled shepherds.

But it was not just literal shepherds and literal flock who were referred to as shepherds and sheep in the Old Testament. This is to say that shepherds and their flocks in the Old Testament were used as metaphors for the Israelites and their leaders. We look at this usage in more detail below.

2. Dynamics of the Metaphor of Shepherds and Flocks
Insights by virtue of analogies

The key to knowledge generated by metaphors lies in analogies;[1] the similarities created or presupposed between the literal context of a concept and the context to which it is applied. A metaphor would break down if there were no perceived similarities between the literal context of a concept, and the context to which it was applied. And so in the Old Testament we have the presupposition of similarities between shepherds in pastoral contexts and leaders in non-pastoral contexts, and between the shepherds' flocks in pastoral contexts and the people of Israel in non-pastoral contexts. This metaphor dynamic is demonstrated in the Psalms, for example, where a psalmist likened YHWH to a shepherd when he referred to him as the shepherd of Israel:

---

1. For more see R. Masson, "Analogy and Metaphoric Process," *TS* 62 (2001): 571–596.

> Give ear, O Shepherd of Israel,
>> you who lead Joseph like a flock! (Ps 80:1)

Since God – in a non-pastoral context – was likened to a shepherd, there must have been those who in the same non-pastoral contexts were likened to sheep (i.e. YHWH's flock), which were the Israelites. We take an illustration of this from the Psalms where there is an awareness amongst God's people that they are his sheep:

> For he is our God,
>> and we are the sheep of his pasture,
> and the sheep of his hand. (Ps 95:7; see also 2 Sam 24:17; Ps 100:3; Isa 40:1)

It is through the analogies inherent in metaphors that familiar concepts in literal contexts shed light on other concepts deemed to be similar to them in their contexts of application. In our case, the familiar shepherds and flocks in literal pastoral contexts shed light on leadership and people that correspond to them in Israel's non-pastoral contexts. Thus, the similarities between the literal pastoral context of shepherds and flocks, and the non-pastoral context of Israel, gave insight into the nature and character of Israel's leaders and her people.

Leaders and followers from a pastoral context

In referring to Israel's leaders as shepherds, the pastoral responsibilities of shepherds were brought to bear upon the Israelites' understanding of their leaders. The people of Israel then conceptualized their leaders pastorally. As a result, just as shepherds were responsible for their flocks, Israel's leaders were understood to have been given the responsibility of leading and protecting God's people. The best example of this comes from Psalm 23 in which YHWH was understood as the leader *par excellence*. Like a shepherd, God led the psalmist towards pastures green and clean waters, and away from danger. He also protected him from evil. However, the pastures to which YHWH was to lead Israel to feed were metaphorically knowledge of his word: "I will give you shepherds after my own heart, who will feed you with knowledge and understanding" (Jer 3:15). More precisely, as suggested by Holladay, shepherds were to feed the Israelites skilfully with knowledge.[2] Justice is also another metaphorical pasture with which Israel was to be fed (Ezek 34:16).

---

2. William L. Holladay, *Jeremiah 1: A Commentary on the Book of the Prophet Jeremiah Chapters 1–25*, Hermenia (Philadelphia: Fortress Press, 1986), 60.

In summary, sheep need pasture to live, and so, when the Israelites were likened to sheep, then ideas of knowledge and justice were the pasture which the people of Israel needed to live. Israel's leaders were responsible to lead the Israelites to this "pasture" (i.e. to give them knowledge and justice).

Furthermore, the proclivities of sheep on account of their nature were brought to bear in understanding the problems of the people of Israel. Thus, like sheep, the Israelites could go astray (Isa 53:6; see also 2 Chr 33:9; Ps 95:10). They also strayed away metaphorically from God's ways through disobedience (Amos 2:4). And like sheep, the Israelites could be led astray: "My people have been lost sheep; their shepherds have led them astray" (Jer 50:6; see also Isa 3:12; 9:16; Jer 23:13; Ezek 13:10; 44:10; 48:11; Amos 2:4; Mic 3:5). But sheep that go astray can be found, and so Israel, like sheep, could also be found (Ezek 34:11–16).

Lastly, like sheep, the people of Israel could also be injured, or wounded, and therefore have their injuries bound (Ezek 34:16; see also Zech 11:16). The Israelites' broken hearts (*lenišebēri lēb*, to which we shall return later) were likened to injuries that in sheep would need to be bound by a shepherd:

> He heals the brokenhearted,
>   and binds up their wounds. (Ps 147:3)

Having established the function of shepherd and sheep metaphors, we are now in a position to examine in some detail the Old Testament's writings on Israel's leaders and their responsibilities to Israel in terms dictated by the metaphor.

3. YHWH, the Shepherd of Israel

Despite having human leaders, YHWH the God of Israel was, as their king, their ultimate leader. This understanding is seen in Deuteronomy where it is stated that God became the king of the Israelites (referred to as Jeshurun – see also Deut 32; Isa 44:2) when their covenant with him was inaugurated:

> The LORD came from Sinai,
>   and dawned from Seir upon us;
> ... Moses charged us with the law,
>   as a possession for the assembly of Jacob.
> Thus YHWH became king in Jeshurun when the heads of the
>   people gathered,
>   the united tribes of Israel. (Deut 33:1–5, RSV and ESV)

The recognition of YHWH as Israel's king is also clear in the story of Gideon. When the people of Israel wanted to make him their king and establish a monarchy, he rejected their intentions because he understood God to be their leader (Judg 8:22–23). We have in the Psalms as well awareness, and praises therefore, of God's kingship over Israel (see Pss 47:6–7; 44:4; 48:2; 74:12; 89:18; 98:6).

That God was the ultimate leader of Israel is also clarified when the people of Israel requested a king (1 Sam 8:5). In requesting a king, Israel was rejecting YHWH as their ruler, and rejecting his kingship over them: "and the LORD said to Samuel, 'Listen to the voice of the people in all that they say to you; for they have not rejected you, but they have rejected me from being king over them'" (1 Sam 8:7; see also 1 Sam 12:12).

Since the Israelites recognized YHWH as their ultimate leader they therefore metaphorically understood him as their shepherd (Ps 80:1) and even entreated him as such in their time of need (Ps 28:9; Mic 7:14). As Israel's shepherd YHWH would have the following pastoral responsibilities over them: (a) leading them to pastures and rest, (b) seeking the lost ones, (c) binding and healing the wounded amongst them, and (d) protecting them from harm and saving them from their enemies. In the Old Testament, we come across the way YHWH intended to fulfil pastorally these four responsibilities through their metaphorical likeness. We turn now to identify those likenesses in order to discuss YHWH's intended shepherding of Israel.

God's word as pasture

We start with examining the pasture with which God would feed the Israelites. God's word, *dabar* (also referred to as commandments [*miswāh*], law or instruction [*torah*] or statutes [*huqqāh*]) to the people of Israel was likened to pasture, or the fold. Pasture gave life to sheep, and so would Israel's keeping of God's word. The linkage of life with obedience to God's laws is set out in Deuteronomy where we read that YHWH promised his people life if they obeyed him. The life he promised was manifest in the blessings they would have from him if they obeyed:

> See, I have set before you life and good, death and evil. If you obey the commandments of the LORD your God . . . then you shall live and multiply and the LORD your God will bless you in the Land that you are entering to take possession of it. (Deut 30:16)

The outcome of the blessings – for example, health longevity, abundance, and security (Deut 28:1–14; see also Lev 26:3–13) – would be abundant life. We see this state of affairs in the lesson YHWH gave Israel about life from obedience, as explained to them by Moses. Moses told them that God's miraculous provision of food when they complained for lack of bread was to teach them that their problem was not following God's word which was essential for living: "one does not live by bread alone but by every that comes from the mouth of the LORD" (Deut 8:3).

This same outlook is also corroborated in the metaphors of Isaiah 55:1–3 whereby YHWH called on the hungering Israelites in Babylon (see Lam 1:11) to come to him for food and drink that required no money to buy.[3] The food and drink, however, was YHWH's word which they were instructed to buy by listening attentively to it so as to follow it:

> Ho, everyone who thirsts,
>   come to the waters;
> and you that have no money,
>   come, buy and eat!
> Come, buy wine and milk
>   without money and without price:
> Why do you spend your money,
>   for that which is not bread,
> and your labour
>   for that which does not satisfy?
> Listen carefully to me,
>   and eat what is good,
>   and delight yourselves in rich food.
> Incline your ear, and come to me;
>   listen, so that you may live. (Isa 55:13)

Sheep without pasture would end up dying, and so would Israel if they disobeyed God's laws. YHWH through Moses promised his people death and evil if they disobeyed his word. Death was also manifest in the curses that would ensue on the land. The outcome of the curses – such as vulnerability, diseases, and scarcity (Deut 28:15–68; see also Lev 26:14–39) – would be death.

This relationship between not following God's word, which is tantamount to not having it, and death, is also encapsulated more directly in the word of

---

3. For more on the metaphors, see Marjo C. A. Korpel, "Metaphors in Isaiah LV," *VT* 46, no. 1 (1996): 49–50.

YHWH through Amos. Through Amos God promised the people of Israel that they would perish in times to come not because of a lack of food but due to a lack of his words.

> The time is surely coming, says the Lord God,
>   when I will send a famine on the land;
> not a famine of bread, or a thirst for water,
>   but of hearing the words of the LORD:
> They shall wander from sea to sea,
>   and from north to east;
> they shall run to and fro,
>   seeking the word of the LORD,
> but they shall not find it
> . . .
> they shall fall, and never rise again. (Amos 8:11–14)

Justice as pasture

As previously established, justice (*tsedek* or *mišpat*)[4] to the people of Israel was also metaphorically likened to pasture. This is clear in God's promise to the Israelites that, as their shepherd, he would feed them with justice: "I will seek the lost and I will bring back the strayed, and I will bind up the injured . . . I will feed them with justice" (Ezek 34:16). Like pasture that gave life to the sheep, justice would give life to the Israelites. However, as we will make clear below, this was through the protection of the life of the weak among the people of Israel.

I have argued extensively elsewhere that justice is central to God's kingship.[5] Psalm 97:2 best captures this by showing that God's throne was founded on justice:

> The LORD is king! Let the earth rejoice;
>   let the many coastlands be glad!
> Clouds and thick darkness are round him;
>   *righteousness and justice are the foundation of his*
>   *throne.* . . . (Ps 97:1–2, my emphasis; see also 89:14)

---

4. We should note that justice (*mišpat*) and righteousness (*tsedek*) are synonymous. I have preferred to use justice, rather than righteousness, because it is the one used mostly in biblical literature.

5. Peter Nyende, *God's Dwelling and Kingdom: A Christian Biblical Theology* (Carlisle: Langham Global Library, 2023), 80–87.

If justice is the foundation of YHWH's throne, then his kingship is based on justice. In addition, YHWH "loves righteousness and justice" (Pss 33:5; 37:28; 99:4; see also Isa 61:8), and he is "a God of justice" (Isa 30:18; Job 37:23).

But YHWH's justice in the Old Testament was a particular kind of justice, namely, social justice. This justice was concerned particularly with protecting the weak from the strong. For this reason it was dual in nature, delivering justice to the weak and meting out punishment to the powerful. This dual nature of God's justice was proclaimed by a psalmist:

> it is God who executes judgement,
>> putting down one and lifting another. (Ps 75:7)

God's justice as social justice is also revealed in places where his justice is elaborated. A psalmist in his praise of YHWH's kingship, for example, portrays his justice as social justice:

> Who is like the LORD our God,
>> who is seated on high:
>
> . . .
>
> He raises the poor from dust,
>> He gives the barren woman a home
> making her the joyous mother of children. (Ps 113:5–9; see also Pss 76:9; 82:2–4)

God's promise to Ezekiel 34 to feed his flock with justice was in essence about social justice. As pointed out by Block:

> The last two statements in v. 16 are difficult, but it seems that the rulers were not only exploiting the weak. The fat (*hăzāqâ*), that is, the bullies within the population, are hereby forewarned that Yahweh *will police* them and *tend them with justice*. On the basis of vv. 17–22, with which the term *mispat* provides an obvious link, Yahweh's action involves imposing restraints on the healthier members of the flock to prevent them from misusing their superior strength against the weaker sheep.[6]

In this sense YHWH's justice, like pasture for sheep, would contribute to giving life to the weak amongst his people which was being sucked away by their enslavement by the powerful or destroyed at their hands.

---

6. Daniel I. Block, *The Book of Ezekiel Chapters 25–48*, NICOT (Grand Rapids: Eerdmans, 1998), 292.

Disobedience as wandering astray

We have already established that the proclivity of sheep to wander was brought to bear on the people of Israel who were likened to sheep. Like sheep they could be led astray or wander away from the fold. The going astray of the Israelites, or their being led astray, was related to God's word; they went astray when they did not, for whatever reason, follow God's word. In some instances, they were understood to have gone astray by outrightly rejecting YHWH's law for lies:

> They have rejected the law of the LORD,
> and have not kept his statutes,
>> but they have been led astray by the same lies
>> after which their ancestors walked. (Amos 2:4)

In other instances they were led astray by following the word of Baal (Jer 23:13), or another idol (Ezek 44:10; Hos 4:12), instead of the word of YHWH. They were also led astray by following the lies they were given in the place of YHWH's word (see Ezek 13:10 and Mic 3:5). This being the case, seeking and finding the lost Israelites would be likened to either giving the word of YHWH, or helping them to follow it. As their shepherd, YHWH would, therefore, do one of the two when he promised that he would himself seek the lost Israelites and bring them back, as is clear in this poignant promise to the Israelites by YHWH himself:

> For thus says the LORD God; *I myself will search for my sheep and will seek them out* ... and I will feed them on the mountains of Israel, by the water courses, and in all the inhabited parts of the land ... and I will make them lie down, say the Lord God. *I will seek the lost, and I will bring back the strayed.* (Ezek 34:11–16, my emphasis)

Indeed, in a psalmist's prayer, best understood against the background of sheep-shepherd metaphor, the psalmist likens disobedience to God's word directly to wandering away from God's way. To walk in God's way was to obey his word which was truth, to disobey God's word was the opposite: to wander away from the path. This is what the psalmist was praying not to do:

> Teach me your way, O LORD,
> that I may walk in your truth. (Ps 86:11)

Comfort as binding wounded sheep

We turn now our attention to what was likened to binding wounded sheep in the shepherding of Israel. Comfort (*naḥam*) in the Old Testament is associated with regret, anxiety, anguish, grief, sorrow, and such like emotions – all bitter and agonizing emotions brought about by difficult or traumatic events or circumstances. To give one relief from any of them is to give comfort. So, for example, by marrying Rebecca Isaac was comforted, relieved of the sorrow of losing his mother (Gen 24:67; see also Gen 38:12; 2 Sam 12:24). Now, YHWH was the comforter of Israel. It was his role to comfort the Israelites: "I am he who comforts you" (Isa 51:12). For this reason God himself, according to his pleasure and unhindered power, would comfort the Israelites when he restored them:

> For the LORD will comfort Zion;
>   he will comfort all her waste places,
> and he will make her wilderness like Eden. (Isa 51:3; see also
>   Isa 12:1; 49:13; 52:9; 66:13; Jer 31:13)

It was in view of YHWH's role as the comforter of Israel that a psalmist cried to him for salvation from his enemies in the confidence that he would grant it – as he had previously done – thereby offering him comfort:

> O God, the insolent rise up against me;
>   a band of ruffians seek my life
> . . .
> Show me a sign of your favour,
> so that those who hate me may see it and be put to shame,
> because you, LORD, have helped me and comforted me.
>   (Ps 86:14–17)

We should note here that words play a big role in giving comfort by expressing care and concern, enlightening, reassuring, strengthening, and leading. Words can comfort the distressed by promising them that their difficult circumstances will be removed, or are transitory in nature. We witness this observation in the narrative of Job where Job's comfort was central on account of his misfortune. Job was unhappy with his friends whom he branded "miserable comforters" (Job 16:2) because their words, being false, did nothing to comfort him, to strengthen or reassure him (Job 21:34; see also Gen 50:21). The role of words in giving comfort is also seen in the same narrative when Job parallels God's comfort with words (Job 15:11). We also witness the role of words in offering comfort in the confession of a prophet, who asserts that his ability to comfort using words was based on the type of tongue which YHWH had given him:

> The LORD God has given me
> the tongue of a teacher
> and skill to console the weary;
> with a word in the morning. (Isa 50:4 NEB)

But why exactly was YHWH's comfort of the Israelites likened to the pastoral responsibility of a shepherd binding and healing wounded sheep? Our answer stems from the reference of binding broken hearts, which denotes offering comfort. In Old Testament literature we come across different modes of expression that include bodily parts as well as emotions. Although contemporary language may still reproduce Old Testament thought and expression, the mode of expression can be antiquated. Considering phrases within the context of Old Testament literature is then the path to understanding them. A broken heart or broken hearts (*šabar lēb*) is one such expression by which is meant regret, or anxiety, or anguish, or grief, or sorrow, or any such like emotions we earlier mentioned brought about by difficult or traumatic events or circumstances.

We come across the broken heart (*šabarā lēbi*) in the cry of a psalmist:

> Insults have broken my heart, so that I am in despair:
> I looked for pity, but there was none;
> and for comforters, but I found none. (Ps 69:20)

The description of the psalmist's circumstances points to the difficult times he experienced, particularly, insults. Insults bring about grief, anguish, sorrow or the like, here expressed as *šabarā lēbi*. In plain language, this psalmist cried out that the insults aimed at him had brought him grief.

Another psalmist cried out to God concerning his broken heart (*nišbar lēb*): "a broken and contrite heart, O God, you will not despise" (Ps 51:17). The context of this cry was David's adultery and "murder," and this points to *nišbar lēb* denoting bitter emotions of regret. David pleaded to God for forgiveness in confidence that God would not disregard his plea because he regretted his sins.

We also come across a broken heart (*nišbar lēbi*) in the cry of the prophet Jeremiah (Jer 23:9). The prophet talked of his broken heart on account of YHWH's prospective judgement of the prophets and priests who had failed in their roles. The prospects of their destruction as a judgment from God was difficult for Jeremiah and must have made him anxious and sorrowful, which he described as a broken heart. In plain language then, Jeremiah cried that he was fearful and sorrowful because of the kind of punishment God promised he would administer on the prophets and priests (Jer 23:9–15).

Understanding *šabar lēb* as denoting the bitter or agonizing emotions experienced by a person due to difficult circumstances helps us to understand why the needy and the brokenhearted (*nikēh lebāb*) are lumped together in Psalm 109. They have in common difficult circumstances, which accounts for the parallelism in Psalm 109:16. To both, the wicked person was unkind, and did not sympathize with their situation:

> For he did not remember to show kindness,
>   but pursued the poor and needy and the brokenhearted
>   to their death. (Ps 109:16)

With the above perspective, we can now grasp why binding and/or healing is twinned with offering comfort. Given the bitter and agonizing emotions encumbering them, they are the ones whom YHWH comforts, the ones he binds and heals, as expressed by a certain psalmist:

> He heals the brokenhearted,
>   and binds up their wounds. (Ps 147:3)

Thus binding and/or healing the brokenhearted was the equivalent to offering comfort to those who needed it. Indeed, this outlook is found in Isaiah where to heal the brokenhearted is to offer comfort:

> I have seen their ways, but I will heal them,
>   I will lead them, and repay them with comfort. (Isa 57:18)

Binding and/or healing as a pastoral language coming from the shepherding responsibility of binding wounded sheep strongly suggests that YHWH's binding of the brokenhearted was its metaphorical likeness. Wounded sheep needed their wounds bound in order to heal, and so did the brokenhearted Israelites need YHWH's binding to recover strength to continue facing life, rather than be crushed by their emotions or their prevailing harsh circumstances. They would be relieved through God's comfort of the often debilitating bitter and agonizing emotions brought about by their difficult circumstances.

We finish our look at the metaphorical likeness of the four pastoral responsibilities in the shepherding of Israel by YHWH by considering what was analogous to protecting and rescuing sheep. It seems clear that the security that YHWH would guarantee the Israelites was likened to protecting and rescuing sheep: "The LORD will cause your enemies who rise against you to be defeated before you" (Deut 28:7). However, as the words of Moses made clear in Deuteronomy 28:1, their protection was contingent on their obedience. This protection from aggressors and enemies was on account of God being their king (shepherd), as confirmed in one Psalm which credited God for Israel's victories due to his kingship:

> For the LORD, the Most High, is awesome,
>   a great king over all the earth:
> He subdued peoples under us,
>   and nations under our feet. (Ps 47:2–3)

4. The Shepherds of Israel

In this section, we examine the designated human shepherds of Israel with respect to their metaphorical shepherding responsibilities of feeding God's flock with knowledge, and with justice, binding the brokenhearted, and protecting them from their enemies. This is because YHWH undertook these pastoral responsibilities he had over Israel through them.

Priest and prophets, feeding God's people, seeking the lost

We begin by looking at Israel's human shepherds whom God chose for the pastoral responsibility of feeding his flock. The metaphorical likeness of pasture to sheep, as we previously saw, was God's word, which when followed would give life to his people. God designated priests and prophets to make known to the Israelites his word that they may follow it and live.

In Old Testament literature, priests were appointed by God (Exod 28:1; Num 18:7–8). They were supposed to give God's words to the people by means of some physical object called "the Urim and Thummim" (Deut 33:8). Due to a lack of information from the Old Testament Scriptures themselves as well as comparative literature, we do not know exactly what these objects were. But we know that as their bearers, priests were to reveal the word of YHWH to people (Exod 28:30; Lev 8:8). It was accordingly expected that the people of Israel would approach priests for YHWH's word: "he shall stand before Eliazar the priest, who shall inquire for him by the decision of the Urim before the LORD" (Num 27:21; see also 1 Sam 28:6; Ezra 2:63). Besides the Urim and Thummim, priests also gave knowledge of God's law to the Israelites by teaching about them: "you are to teach the people of Israel all the statutes that the LORD has spoken to them through Moses" (Lev 10:11; see also Deut 33:10; Ezek 44:23–24; Mal 2:7). They would also generally, "handle the law" (Jer 2:8; also Jer 18:18), by which must have been meant forms of verbal delivery, including teaching, of God's word to his people.

It is in view of their pastoral responsibility to feed God's people with knowledge of his word that God declared imminent judgement on priests for their failure to do so:

> My people are destroyed for lack of knowledge;
>   because you have rejected knowledge,
> I reject you from being a priest to me:
> And since you have forgotten the law of your God,
>   I will also forget your children. (Hos 4:6)

As for the prophets, they were called by God to be his spokespersons. This understanding is manifest in the Exodus narrative when YHWH told Moses that Aaron would be his prophet because he would speak what Moses told him to (i.e. be Moses's spokesman):

> See, I have made you like God to Pharaoh, and your brother Aaron shall be your prophet. You shall speak all I command you and your brother Aaron shall tell Pharoah. (Exod 7:1–2)

Such was the expectation that the test of a true prophet was the coming to pass of what they declared was YHWH's word. YHWH was almighty, and so would always bring to pass what he said. He was also foreknowing, telling, for example, the end from the beginning. In the light of YHWH's nature, a true prophet's word would not fail to come to pass for it was YHWH's: "If a prophet speaks in the name of the LORD but the thing does not take place or prove true, it is a word the LORD has not spoken" (Deut 18:22). This is why the people of Israel expected prophets to give them God's word except when they were in a state of rebellion. Then they would request the prophets not to tell them what God was saying (Isa 30:10).

For these reasons, prophets who failed, and worse, misled God's people were, according to the law, liable to death (Deut 13:1–5). Indeed YHWH through the prophets declared judgement on the prophets for the same reasons:

> The word of the LORD came to me: Mortal, prophesy against the prophets of Israel who are prophesying; say to those who prophesy out of their imagination: "Hear the word of the LORD!" Thus says the LORD God, Alas for the senseless prophets who follow their own spirits, and have nothing! . . . Therefore thus says the LORD God: Because you have uttered falsehood and prophesied lies, I am against you, says the LORD God. My hand will be against the

prophets who see false visions and utter lying divinations; they shall not be in the council of my people, nor be enrolled in the register of the houses of Israel. (Ezek 13:1–9; see also Ezek 22:28; Jer 5:12–13; 23:31–32; Isa 9:15)

Thus, just like priests, prophets were given the pastoral responsibility to give the Israelites knowledge of God's word that they may follow it to live. Since both priests and prophets were Israel's human prophets who shared the pastoral responsibility of feeding God's people with knowledge of his word, they were lumped together for failing to do so:

> prophets prophesy lies
>   and priests go hand in hand with them,
> and my people love to have it so.
> How will you fare at the end of it all? (Jer 5:31 NEB; see also
>   Jer 6:13; 23:11; 26:11; Mic 3:11; Isa 28:7–8)

The promise of YHWH to give the Israelites good shepherds also conflated the two types of leaders. Reference to the coming good shepherds feeding the people with knowledge and understanding was in contradistinction to both priests and prophets who, as bad shepherds, had failed to feed God's people knowledge of his word: "I will give you shepherds after my own heart, who will feed you with knowledge and understanding" (Jer 3:15). It should therefore be no surprise that the Israelites identified the two with words directly from YHWH: "for the law shall not perish from the priest, nor counsel from the wise, nor the word from the prophet" (Jer 18:18 ESV; see also Ezek 7:26).

God also gave these two groups of shepherds the pastoral responsibility to seek and find the lost Israelites. Since, as we pointed out, the Israelites went astray when they did not follow God's law, it was priests and prophets who were to seek them and bring them back to the fold by giving them knowledge of God's law or helping them to follow it. God was displeased with these shepherds for their failure to do so: "you have not brought back the strayed, you have not sought the lost" (Ezek 34:4).

Kings and feeding God's people with justice

We turn now to examine another group of Israel's human shepherds whom God chose for the pastoral responsibility of feeding his flock, not with knowledge of his laws but with justice. We earlier pointed out that justice, along with knowledge of God's word, were the metaphorical likeness of pasture. God designated the Davidic kings (King David and his progeny on his throne) to carry out this pastoral responsibility. They were chosen by God to shepherd his people when he chose David (see 2 Sam 7:11–16) and his lineage to rule over Israel as highlighted in Old Testament literature:

> He chose his servant David,
>   and took him from the sheepfolds;
> from tending the nursing ewes he brought him
>   to be the shepherd of his people Jacob,
>   of Israel, his inheritance (Ps 78:70–71; see also Ps 89:3, 19; 1 Kgs 8:16)

We pointed out that justice was central to YHWH's kingship. This justice was dual in nature for it was concerned with offering the weak justice and punishing the powerful for their injustices. The Davidic kings were designated to deliver this type of justice in line with God's commandments. Their pastoral responsibility to deliver social justice is clearly stated in God's word through the prophet Jeremiah when he warned the Davidic kings of dire penalties if they failed to give justice to the weak:

> Hear the word of the LORD, O King of Judah sitting on the throne of David – you, and your servants, and your people who enter these gates. Thus says the LORD: Act with justice and righteousness, and deliver from the hand of the oppressor anyone who has been robbed. And do not wrong or violence to the alien, the orphan, and the widow, or shed innocent blood in this place. (Jer 22:2–3; see also Jer 21:11–12)

This pastoral responsibility is also clear in the Psalms. A psalmist prayed for a Davidic king to be empowered to give social justice (Ps 72:1–4). The pastoral responsibility of the Davidic kings to execute social justice is found as well in God's promises of the restoration of Israel. YHWH pointed out that the Davidic king through whose enthronement he promised to restore the kingship would, in contradistinction to others in the past, deliver social justice by observing the Jubilee laws and the sabbatical years both of which were concerned exclusively with justice for the weak (Isa 61:1–2).

The promised Davidic king would deliver social justice in absolute terms, because he would give it with complete knowledge of the circumstances of the weak:

> He shall not judge by what his eyes see,
>   or decide by what his ears hear;

> but with righteousness he shall judge the poor,
> and decide with equity for the meek of the earth.
> (Isa 11:3–4)

God also said through Isaiah that the promised Davidic king would effectively offer social justice because his rule would be grounded in justice (Isa 9:6).

Moreover, it seems that through the promised Davidic king, God would assume himself the pastoral responsibility of feeding his people with justice. This outlook is based on God's promise to remove failed human shepherds and become himself the good shepherd of Israel. As a consequence, he would fulfil the pastoral responsibility of feeding them with justice in contrast to Israel's kings who failed in that responsibility:

> I myself will be the shepherd of my sheep, and I will make them lie down, says the LORD God. I will seek the lost, and I will bring back the strayed, and I will bind up the injured, and *I will strengthen the weak, but the fat and the strong I will destroy. I will feed them with justice.* (Ezek 34:15–16, my emphasis)

Prophets and binding the wounded

Next for consideration are the human shepherds whom God chose for the pastoral responsibility to bind and/or heal the injured of his flock. The metaphorical likeness of binding wounded sheep, as we pointed out earlier, was comforting the anxious, grieving, sorrowful, etc, or, to use the biblical expression, binding the brokenhearted. It is apparent in Old Testament literature that God designated prophets to shoulder this responsibility as epitomized in YHWH's instructions to the prophet to comfort the people of Israel (Isa 40:1).

The basis for placing this shepherding responsibility on prophets lay in their calling as God's spokespersons in a most direct way. Through the prophets, God was not simply having his word generally proclaimed to the people but would do so in ways specific to their circumstances, and/or thoughts and emotions. A prophet's word could thereby lead them (enlightening or telling them what they must do), or reveal God's plans to them (telling them of what God was doing and/or going to do about their difficult circumstances – see Amos 3:7), or both. Since a leading or revelatory word was timely, the prophets could give God's timely word to his people. This is precisely the success of the prophet we mentioned earlier who had been given a tongue to console. In the words of Baltzer:

What is said makes clear that the one who is introducing himself here is a "teacher." His function is to speak and listen. He himself a "disciple," "a scholar," (לִמּוּד) and he passes on that which he has heard from his Lord and master. He is not just any teacher, he has a direct relationship to God himself.[7]

Some prophets took advantage of this expectation to deceive for gain God's people:

> Thus says the LORD concerning the prophets
> who lead my people astray, who cry "Peace"
>   when they have something to eat,
> but declare war against those
>   who put nothing into their mouths:
> Therefore it shall be night to you. (Mic 3:5–7)

God's timely word enabled the prophets to offer comfort to God's people. We have three clear indications of this phenomenon in Isaiah, Jeremiah, and Zechariah. In Isaiah, the prophet is instructed to comfort his people through YHWH's timely word, which is the revelation that their judgement is over (Isa 40:1–2). YHWH's word through the prophet was related to their immediate circumstances of suffering. It would have comforted them because of the promise that their suffering had come to an end. If we go back to the equivalent biblical expression, the prophet would have fulfilled his pastoral responsibility of binding the brokenhearted Israelites through the comforting words from YHWH.

In Jeremiah YHWH lamented that the prophets of Israel failed in their pastoral responsibility of binding and healing the brokenhearted. Rather than striving to give them God's timely word to bind their broken hearts, they lied to them to no effect. Their promises (allegedly from YHWH) could not bring healing to their broken hearts because they were lies, and not revelations from God to give the people comfort:

> They have treated the wound of my people carelessly,
>   saying, "Peace, peace," when there is no peace. (Jer 8:11)

In Zechariah, YHWH, through the prophet, charged the prophets for not fulfilling their shepherding responsibility of comforting his people because they uttered falsities; words that were neither from YHWH nor timely. For that reason, they offered empty consolations:

---

7. Klaus Baltzer, *Deutero-Isaiah: A Commentary on Isaiah 40–55*, Hermeneia (Philadelphia: Fortress Press, 2001), 339.

> For teraphim utter nonsense
> >   and the diviners see lies;
> > the dreamers tell false dreams,
> >   and give empty consolation:
> > Therefore the people wander like sheep;
> >   they suffer for lack of a shepherd. (Zech 10:2)

Another basis for viewing the prophets as designated for the pastoral responsibility of comforting God's people was in their implicit role of healing and the miraculous. This role is evident in the non-literary prophets Elijah and Elisha by virtue of God using them for healing and for other miraculous deeds, for the sake of his people. The words of Elisha in response to the request from Syria to the king of Israel for the healing of Naaman, who commanded the army of the Syrian king, capture clearly this implied role. Israel's king, Jehoshaphat, could not heal Naaman as requested by Naaman's king, but Elijah could because he was a prophet, so Elijah sent King Jehoshaphat a message not to worry saying: "Let him [Naaman] come to me, that he may learn that there is a prophet in Israel" (2 Kgs 5:8). Healing and other miraculous deeds, just as giving God's word, were also, therefore, a prophet's role. As such, a prophet could offer comfort to the suffering, anguished, or mourning, by miraculous acts that removed their difficult circumstances of illness (see 2 Kgs 5:3), or some hardship (1 Kgs 17:8–16; 2 Kgs 4:1–7; 4:42–44), or even death (1 Kgs 17:17–24; 2 Kgs 4:32–37).

We finish our look at the human shepherds whom God chose to use for various shepherding responsibilities by looking at the ones whom God chose to protect his flock. The metaphorical likeness of protecting and rescuing sheep from predators, we pointed out, was the security of the people of Israel. God designated the Davidic kingship for the pastoral responsibility of protecting his people from their enemies.

One of the promises given to the Davidic kingship was that the kingship would prevail over their enemies: "The enemy shall not outwit him . . . I will crush his foes before him" (Ps 89:20–23; see also Pss 110:2; 132:18). In one psalm, a psalmist (in a context that points to "my lord" being a Davidic king) heard YHWH instruct his lord to sit at his right hand. The reason for seating at YHWH's right hand was for the Davidic king to subdue his enemies:

> The LORD says to my lord,
> >   "Sit at my right hand
> > until I make your enemies your footstool." (Ps 110:1)

Since the Davidic kings were the rulers of Israel, triumphing over their enemies ensured the protection of God's flock and would guarantee life and peace. This perspective enlightens the prayers of a psalmist for a Davidic king (Ps 72:1–11) associating him with peace on the land: "In his days may . . . peace abound" (Ps 72:7). Without the king defeating Israel's enemies, God's flock would not have life and peace as a consequence, and so the psalmist accordingly offered his prayers (Ps 72:9; see also Ps 20:6–9). However, just as knowledge of God's word would be like pasture to God's people when they followed it, protection of God's people would be forthcoming from the Davidic kings when they ruled according to God's wishes (Deut 17:18–20).

5. Jesus, the Shepherd of Israel

In the narrative of the Gospel according to Matthew, it is written of Jesus, when King Herod inquires about the birth place of the promised Davidic king, that he would shepherd (*poimanei*) the people of Israel:

> They told him,
> "In Bethlehem, of Judea; for so it has been written by the prophet:
>> And you, Bethlehem, in the land of Judah,
> are by no means least among the rulers of Judah;
>> for from you shall come a ruler
>> who is to shepherd my people Israel." (Matt 2:5–6)

As is clear by virtue of the Old Testament quotation, the proper perspective for this revelation is the Old Testament. The identity of Jesus as a shepherd in the gospel is the culmination of the story of the Old Testament concerning Israel's human shepherds. Israel's shepherds, as we have alluded, failed in their respective pastoral responsibilities. For that reason, they were punished, together with the flock they were responsible for, with near destruction but for a remnant. Subsequent to their punishment, God promised them that they would have good shepherds, a Davidic king who would be a good shepherd because he would rule in justice, and they would even have God himself as their shepherd. In Jesus Christ the promises to Israel of having good shepherds, and *a* good shepherd, are fulfilled; indeed according to the Gospel of John, Jesus referred to himself as the good shepherd (John 10:11). God therefore designated Jesus for the pastoral responsibilities over Israel which he had earlier given to priests, prophets, and the Davidic kingship.

It is important to note here that the pastoral responsibilities of the human shepherds of Israel were of two kinds: the executive and the non-executive. The executive ones have to do with rule. They were accordingly limited to the Davidic kingship whom God chose to rule Israel as their kings and thus lords (*adonai*). These were the delivery of justice and the protection of God's people. The non-executive ones were the non-ruling ones; they were the ones carried out by the priests and prophets as we have shown with respect to making known God's word, by prophets with respect to binding the brokenhearted, and, by priests, as we shall demonstrate in Chapter 5, with respect to facilitating worship in the temple. Jesus's pastoral responsibilities according to the Gospels combined both of them. As it were, he was king, prophet, and priest. This is best indicated in the prophecy in Isaiah 61 which captures both the executive and non-executive pastoral responsibilities in the promise of a royal prophet. Jesus himself declared that the two were his pastoral responsibilities as the shepherd of Israel before he commenced his work according to Luke's gospel:

> The spirit of the LORD God is upon me,
> > because the LORD has anointed me;
> he has sent me to bring good news to the oppressed,
> > to bind up the brokenhearted
> to proclaim liberty to the captives,
> > and release to the prisoners;
> to proclaim the year of the LORD's favour,
> > and the day of vengeance of our God;
> to comfort all who mourn. (Isa 61:1–2; see Luke 4:18–19)

Since Jesus exclusively reigned as the promised Davidic king and continued to do so after his death and resurrection, his executive pastoral responsibilities were not shared with, nor taken up by, his disciples as part of their pastoral responsibilities. They therefore cannot be viewed as integral to Jesus's shepherding responsibilities that were shared with, and passed on to, his disciples. It would then follow that reference to Jesus as the chief shepherd (*tou archipoimenos*) in the first letter of Peter (1 Pet 5:4) is limited to his non-executive pastoral responsibilities. They are therefore the basis for understanding pastoral ministry and will be the focus of our study in the coming chapters.

3

Preaching and Teaching the Word: the Primary Activities in Pastoral Ministry

We commence forging a biblical perspective of pastoral ministry by first examining its most predominant and crucial aspect, namely the primary activities of pastoral ministry which Jesus, the apostles and others carried out according to the New Testament. These primary activities in pastoral ministry are rooted in the pastoral responsibility of the Old Testament priests and prophets. As we pointed out, it was their pastoral responsibility as shepherds of Israel to feed God's people with the knowledge of his word. Since Jesus was both a priest and a prophet, he carried out this pastoral responsibility by preaching and teaching God's word to God's people. He shared this ministry with the twelve apostles, and subsequently left them to carry it out when he physically departed. Indeed, the apostles carried out pastoral ministry as Jesus commissioned them but did so together with others. Before we examine in detail how Jesus carried out these primary activities of pastoral ministry, and how the apostles' and their co-workers replicated them, we must first establish that he was indeed a prophet and a priest according to the New Testament Scriptures.

1. Jesus the Prophet

Through various stories in the Gospels, Jesus himself revealed his status as a prophet. As we noted earlier, Luke narrated how Jesus revealed that he was the royal prophet promised by YHWH in Isaiah when he read the scroll in the synagogue (Luke 4:18–21; see also Luke 7:22). But, there is more from the Gospels; when disbelieved in his home town, Mark and John narrate that Jesus intimated he was a prophet by stating that "Prophets are without honour, except in their hometown, and among their own kin, and in their own house" (Mark 6:4; John 4:43–44). Luke too narrates that Jesus intimated he was a prophet when he alluded to Jerusalem as the city in which he would have to die when he said: "Yet, today, tomorrow, and the next day I must be on my way, because it is impossible for a prophet to be killed away from Jerusalem" (Luke 13:33).

The Gospels also reveal that Jesus was a prophet in narratives where he was referred to as a prophet by those who believed in him. In fact, they believed in him precisely because they recognized that he was a prophet. An example is the account of Jesus's conversation with the Samaritan woman. In this story, she perceived that he was a prophet – "Sir, I see that you are a prophet" (John 4:19) – and subsequently believed in him (John 4:29). The story of Jesus's triumphal entry into Jerusalem is another example. When he entered Jerusalem riding on a donkey, the crowd which welcomed him perceived that he was a prophet: "The crowds were saying, 'This is the prophet Jesus from Nazareth in Galilee'" (Matt 21:11; see also Matt 21:46). Jesus's status as a prophet among believers must have been public to the extent that those who detained him before his crucifixion used it to mock him; while blindfolding him, they struck him while asking him to prophesy who it was that had done so (Mark 14:65; see also Luke 22:64). In John's gospel mention is made that some of those who heard Jesus believed he was the prophet: "When they heard these words, some in the crowd said, 'This is really the prophet'" (John 7:40).

The book of Acts also shows that Jesus was a prophet. The apostles, having been close to Jesus, are reported in one narrative to have pointed out that he was the promised prophet. They preached to the Jews that he was a prophet in fulfilment of Moses's prophecy that God would raise for the Israelites a prophet like him (Acts 3:22; see also Acts 7:27).

2. Jesus the Priest

Concerning Jesus's status as a priest, we have references in the Gospels of him praying (see e.g. Matt 14:23; 19:13; Mark 1:35; 6:46; Luke 22:31–32) that point to his priesthood. However, it is in the Gospel of John albeit, as noted by Heil,[1] in subtle and symbolic ways, that his priesthood is relatively emphasized. First, we have Jesus priesthood revealed through his prayer in John 17. The prayer

---

1. John Paul Heil, "Jesus as the Unique High Priest in the Gospel of John," *CBQ* 57, no. 4 (1995): 729–745, 730.

had three features which cast it as a prayer Jesus offered as a high priest as we explain below.

The first of the three features we examine is its order. This prayer of Jesus is considered a priestly prayer offered by Jesus as a priest on account of the order of its content. Jesus prayed for himself (17:1–5), then interceded for his disciples (John 17:6–19), then concluded by praying for the world, and for those who would come to believe in him through the witness and word of his disciples (John 17:20–26). As noted by a number of biblical scholars[2] this order parallels the pattern of the sequence of sacrifices YHWH commanded the high priest on "the day of atonement," *yom kippur*. He was to offer a sacrifice first for himself, then his house, and finally for the people of Israel (Lev 16:17). For this reason his prayer ought to be understood as the intercession of a high priest in view of his priestly task.

The second feature is the motif of "consecration" (from the Greek verb *hagiazō*) in the content of the prayer. *Hagiazō* literally means "to make holy" and is used in the Greek version of the Old Testament (the LXX) for the setting apart of things for God or for his service in the temple (see Exod 29:1; Lev 21:8; Deut 15:19). Jesus's prayer for his own consecration as well as that of his disciples (John 17:17, 19) invariably evoked, as noted by Attridge, "the realm of the cult (the temple) with its personnel and its offerings" (mine in brackets).[3] This scenario equated the prayer of Jesus to one a priest offered within the temple precincts thereby making it a priestly prayer in fulfilment of the priestly tasks of his pastoral ministry.

The third feature which makes Jesus's prayer a prayer he offered as a priest or high priest has to do with the "name" (*onoma*) of God, the tetragram, YHWH. Jesus prayed that God would manifest his name to his disciples: "I have made your name known to those whom you gave me from the world" (John 17:6). Jesus also prays to God to keep them in his name as he did when he has been with them (John 17:11–12). This content of Jesus's prayers also casts him as a high priest in his priestly task of intercession for the protection of God's people in a way equivalent to the divine name on the signet that was fastened on Aaron's turban (Exod 28:28–38) as a revelation to, and the protection of, God's people (Exod 28:36–38).

---

2. See for example Raymond E. Brown, *The Gospel According to John XIII–XXI*, Vol. 29A, AB (Garden City: Doubleday & Co, 1970); Andre Feuillet, *The Priesthood of Christ and His Ministers*, translated into English by Matthew J. O'Connell (Garden City: Doubleday, 1975); and Harold W. Attridge, "How Priestly Is the 'High Priestly Prayer' of John 17?" *CBQ* 75, no. 1 (2013): 1–14.

3. Attridge, "How Priestly Is the 'High Priestly Prayer' of John 17?" 10.

Jesus is also revealed as a priest in a description of his clothing in John 19:23. Although the narrator points that the soldiers who shared Jesus's garment and cast lots for his tunic was a fulfilment of Psalms 22:18, the description of Jesus's seamless tunic was a subtle revelation of his priesthood:

> When the soldiers had crucified Jesus, they took his clothes and divided them into four parts, one for each soldier. They also took his tunic; now the tunic was seamless, woven in one piece from the top. So they said to one another, "let us not tear it, but cast lots for it to see who will get it." This was to fulfil what the Scripture says,
>
> "They divided my clothes among themselves,
>   and for my clothing they cast lots." (John 19:23–24)

The mention that Jesus's seamless tunic was of one piece from the top revealed that it had similarities with the robes of a high priest since YHWH instructed that the robes of a high priest be woven from the top as a whole (Exod 28:31–32). Given the subtle communication of Jesus's priesthood in John, it is likely that this similarity was not incidental but a deliberate intimation to reveal that Jesus was a priest.

When we consider the Epistles for Jesus's priesthood, we see that Jesus is revealed to be the one who speaks to God on behalf of believers. As the one who makes petition (*entugkanei*) to God for them having died for their sins, no accusation against them can stand: "Who is to condemn? It is Christ Jesus, who died, yes, who was raised, who is at the right hand of God who intercedes for us" (Rom 8:34). Also, believers who sin should not despair, because they have Jesus as the one who pleads their cause (*paraklētos*) before God: "I write this to you so that you will not sin. But if anybody does sin, we have an advocate with the Father – Jesus Christ the Righteous One" (1 John 2:1 NIV).

However, it is in the book of Hebrews that we have an explicit mention in the New Testament of Jesus's status as a priest. In the book, it is revealed that Jesus was appointed a priest by God, but in the type (*taxin*) of Melchizedek, and not of Aaron or Levi:

> So also Christ did not glorify himself in becoming a high priest,
>   but was appointed by the one who said to him,
>
> "You are my Son, today I have begotten you";
>   as he says also in another place,
> "You are a priest forever, according to the order of
>   Melchizedek." (Heb 5:5–6; see also Heb 7:15–17)

3. Jesus's Primary Activities of Pastoral Ministry
Delivering God's word to God's people

Since Jesus was Israel's shepherd in the fashion of a prophet and priest, he fulfilled the shepherds of Israel's non-executive pastoral responsibilities we mentioned in our second chapter. We will thus from here on call those non-executive pastoral responsibilities, "pastoral ministry" because the understanding we shall forge from the New Testament for what we call "pastoral ministry" reflects Old Testament non-executive pastoral responsibilities of prophets and priests. In other words the pastoral responsibilities of prophets and priests in the Old Testament are equivalent to the pastoral ministry of Jesus and the apostles (together with their non-apostolic counterparts) in the New Testament. Furthermore, substituting pastoral ministry for pastoral responsibilities is in order because from around the 1940s, "pastoral ministry" or "ministry" has virtually been the only term used to denote pastoral responsibilities.[4] This is the reason why, as was the case with our introductory chapter, the meaning of the term is usually assumed and thus unstated.

We shall also from here on refer to Jesus as "the pastor of Israel" for, in his capacity as the prophetic and priestly shepherd of Israel, he carried out in his pastoral ministry those shepherds' pastoral responsibilities. Although calling Jesus the pastor of Israel is the logical implication of our Old Testament study, it is in keeping with the reference to Jesus as the chief pastor in 1 Peter 5:4, which has informed our study's approach which is: understanding pastoral ministry based on Jesus's operations as the chief pastor.

The Gospels indeed show that Jesus, as the pastor of Israel, carried out pastoral ministry predominantly by giving God's word to the people of Israel as summarized in Luke where Jesus is talked of as "a prophet mighty in . . . word" (Luke 24:19; see also Matt 13:54; Mark 6:1–2).

The most forthright evidence for Jesus's pastoral ministry of giving God's word to God's people comes from the Gospel of John. There, Jesus is revealed as the divine word (*logos* – John 1:1) who became flesh (John 1:14). The proper context to understand this revelation and its linkage to Jesus's spoken words

---

4. This shift to the usage of the term pastoral ministry for the work of pastors was on account of the interpretation of the New Testament's Greek word *diakonia* (ministry or service) – under the heavy influence of H. W. Beyer's discussion of the word in his theological dictionary of the New Testament of 1935 edited by Gerhard Kittel, *Theologisches Wörterbuch zum Neun Testament* – which engendered the perception of pastoral work as a ministry. A brief critical summary on this can be found in John Collins, "A Monocultural Usage: διακον-words in Classical, Hellenistic, and Patristic Sources," *VigChr* 66 (2012): 290–295.

(*logoi*) as God's word is the Old Testament (as McKenzie argued years ago).[5] Countless times in Old Testament literature a commandment, a promise or promises, a judgement or judgements, a prediction or predictions, a vision or visions etc., that was/were given by God is/are expressed in the singular as "the word (*dabar*) of YHWH" (for example Gen 15:1; Deut 5:5; Exod 9:20; Num 3:16; 1 Sam 3:1; 1 Kgs 22:19; Amos 7:16; Isa 1:10; Jer 1:2; Ezek 3:16). We also have in the Old Testament a shortened form of the word of YHWH in "the word" (Deut 4:2; 30:14; Jer 5:13; 25:1). Accordingly, the word of YHWH was mentioned to him in prayers as "your word," as epitomized in the parallelism of Psalm 119 (Ps 119:9, 16, 17, 25 etc.; see also Pss 130:5; 147:19).

"The word of YHWH" or "the word" was therefore a label for any form of communication that came from God – it signified YHWH's message or messages. This understanding is explicit in John's gospel where "the word" directly referred to God's messages through Jesus: "Whoever does not love me does not keep my words; and *the word* (*ho logos*) you hear is not mine, but is from the Father who sent me" (John 14:24, my emphasis). We also have "the word" understood as God's messages in other New Testament literature as follows: 1. at a home in Capernaum where Jesus was "speaking the Word" (Mark 2:2); 2. by the lake of Gennesaret where crowds milled around him to hear "the word of God" (Luke 5:1); 3. in the parable of the sower where the seed sown on varied ground was likened to "the word" (Mark 4:14–20; Matt 13:18–23; Luke 8:11–15); 4. in Acts where several persons "preached the word" or "the word of the Lord" (Acts 8:4; 13:5; 15:35; 17:13), and "the word of God" was understood to have spread (Acts 6:7; Acts 12:24; Acts 19:20); 5. in the Epistle of Peter where "the word of God" is perceived to bring life (1 Pet 1:23–25); 6. in Hebrews where "the word of God" is said to discern hearts and minds (Heb 4:12; also Heb 6:5); and 7. in James where the audience of the letter are asked to be doers of "the word" (Jas 1:22–23).

The question that forces itself upon us is this: exactly how was Jesus, as the divine word, "the messages of God"? Although John's gospel does not state explicitly how Jesus was "God's messages," it is clear from the rest of the narrative that Jesus was the word through fulfilling the pastoral ministry of giving God's messages to God's people. In the gospel's narrative, Jesus as the divine *logos* unceasingly spoke God's message(s); his spoken words (*logoi*) were the word of God. This relationship between Jesus's words and the word of God is pointed out severally by the narrator's account of Jesus's own explanation which clarified that he, as the divine *logos*, was speaking the word of God:

---

5. John L. McKenzie, "The Word of God in the Old Testament," *TS* 21 (1960): 183–206.

> He whom God has sent speaks the words of God.... (John 3:34)
>
> My teaching is not mine but his who sent me. (John 7:16–17)
>
> I do nothing on my own, but speak these things as the Father instructed me. (John 8:28)
>
> For I have not spoken of my own, but the Father who sent me has himself given me a commandment about what to say and what to speak. (John 12:49)
>
> For the words you gave to me I have given them. (John 17:8)

For this reason the gospel itself is plotted essentially around Jesus's words (his teachings, his "I am" sayings, and his lengthy farewell discourse).

In the Gospel of Matthew, Jesus is also seen as fulfilling the pastoral ministry of giving God's word to God's people. In general terms, the narrative of Matthew's gospel is plotted around five sets of sayings/teachings which conclude, except for his kingdom parables (13:1–52), with the words, "when Jesus had finished these sayings" (*kai egeneto hote etelesan ho Isous* – Matt 5:1–7:28; 10:5–11:1; 13:1–52; 18:1–19:1; 23:1–26:1). Since the contents of Matthew 5 are God's commandments as contained in Mosaic law, it is clear that these sets of sayings were meant to give the Israelites knowledge of God's word. Jesus thereby as the pastor of Israel carried out the pastoral ministry of giving God's word to God's people.

More particularly in Matthew (see Matt 9:35–38), Jesus's work is depicted as one predominated by teaching and preaching which, as we make clear later, was the delivery of God's word: "Then Jesus went about all the cities and villages, teaching in their synagogues, and proclaiming the good news of the kingdom" (Matt 9:35; also Matt 4:23). Of significance was that this delivery of God's word was linked with a shepherd-sheep metaphor (Matt 9:36) thus casting Jesus's teaching as the word of God with which he fed the flock of God.

According to Matthew 9:35–38, Jesus realized during the course of fulfilling his pastoral ministry of giving God's word to God's people that their need for that pastoral ministry was greater than he could meet. He perceived that like sheep without a shepherd the people were bereft of knowledge of the word of God. This lack of knowledge made them vulnerable to undernourishment, and being led astray as indicated in the verbs *eklelumenoi* (troubled/afflicted) and *errimmenoi* (helpless/down) which implied "oppression or exhaustion or lack of direction or probably all of these together."[6] More pastors like him

---

6. R. T. France, *The Gospel of Matthew*, NICNT (Grand Rapids: Eerdmans, 2007), 272.

were therefore needed to carry out this pastoral ministry if the security and health of the people of Israel was to be guaranteed. Jesus therefore asked his disciples to pray that God would send out more pastors (referred to as "labourers" in a sudden switch of metaphor within the same discourse), to execute this pastoral ministry:

> Then Jesus went about all the cities and villages, teaching in their synagogues, and proclaiming the good news of the kingdom, and curing every disease and every sickness. When he saw the crowds, he had compassion for them, because they were harassed (*eklelumenoi*) and helpless (*errimmenoi*), like sheep without a shepherd. Then he said to the disciples, "The harvest is plentiful, but the labourers are few; therefore ask the Lord of the harvest to send out labourers into the harvest. (Matt 9:35–38)

Outside the Gospels we see Jesus's fulfilment of the pastoral ministry of giving God's word to God's people underscored in Hebrews. The writer of the book actually introduced his "word of exhortation" (Heb 13:22) by clarifying to his audience where the most current delivery of God's word lay. Speaking as a Jew, he pointed out that unlike their preceding generations who had God's word given to them by their shepherds, the prophets, God had given his word to his generation through his Son. Jesus was thereby fulfilling a prophetic role: "Long ago God spoke to our ancestors in many and various ways by the prophets, but in these last days he has spoken to us by a Son" (Heb 1:1–2).

From these New Testament writings it is clear that Jesus, as the pastor of Israel, fulfilled the pastoral ministry of giving the word of the Lord to God's people. We now proceed to discuss the two specific ways in which the Gospels enlighten us that he did.

Preaching the word of God

In the Gospels, Jesus's work was characterized by preaching (*kērussōn*) and teaching (*didaskōn*). This scenario is precisely captured in Matthew's account: "Jesus went through Galilee, teaching (*didaskōn*) in their synagogues, and proclaiming (*kērussōn*) the good news of the kingdom . . ." (Matt 4:23). The same description of Jesus's ministry is repeated in Matthew 9:35 and in Matthew 11:1.

In the classic Greek lexicon by Abbott-Smith, the Greek for preaching (*kērussōn*)[7] means to proclaim or announce publicly. In Matthew and Mark, and only once in Luke, Jesus is said to have preached or intended to go preach-

---

7. G. Abbott-Smith, *A Manual Greek Lexicon*, 246.

ing nine times (see for example Matt 4:17; Mark 1:14; and Luke 4:44). *Kērussōn* is semantically almost identical to preaching the good news (*euangelizomenos*),[8] because the latter verb also means to announce or proclaim, but specifically the good news, or even simply to bring good news. In Luke's account Jesus is said to have preached the good news or intended to go preaching the good news four times (Luke 4:43; 7:22; 8:1; 20:1). In the final analysis, "preaching" and "preaching the good news" are synonymous in the Gospels as demonstrated by their interchange to refer to the same activity. So, for example, whereas in Matthew's account Jesus went preaching (*kērussōn*) in towns and villages of Galilee (Matt 9:35), in Luke's account he went preaching the good news (*euangelizomenos*) in those cities and villages (Luke 8:1).

But what exactly was Jesus proclaiming? The use of *euangelizomenos* to describe Jesus's preaching indicates that what Jesus proclaimed was good news; hence, in some instances, the use of simply "good news," *euaggelion* (Matt 26:13; Mark 8:35; 14:9; 16:15), to refer to what he proclaimed. From the Gospels we learn that this good news centred on the kingdom of God: "Jesus went throughout Galilee proclaiming the good news of the kingdom" (Matt 4:23; 9:35; 24:14; Luke 4:43–44; 8:1; 16:16). We also learn from the Gospels that the good news belonged to God, "the good news of God" (Mark 1:14; see also 2 Cor 11:7; 1 Thess 2:9) in the sense of either coming from God or being sent by God. Either way, this meant that the good news which Jesus proclaimed was not his own but the word of God. Let us now briefly discuss this proclamation to clarify this conclusion.

As the pastor of Israel, Jesus's proclamation would not have been his own but God's timely word which he gave to the people of Israel. If we may simplify, God's word through the prophets to Israel in the Old Testament was that the dethroned Davidic kingship would be restored through the *māšiah*, the promised Davidic king. Israel, the temple, and her covenant with God would also be restored. After many years of waiting for the fulfilment of this promise, Jesus appeared and started proclaiming to the Israelites the fulfilment of this word. The Synoptic Gospels' settings, which usher Jesus's proclamation, point toward this view by giving select Old Testament prophecies and presupposing its narrative (Matt 1:1–17; Mark 1:1–14; Luke 1:1–2:40).

> Jesus came to Galilee, proclaiming the good news of God, and saying, "The time is fulfilled, and the kingdom of God has come near; repent, and believe the good news." (Mark 1:14–15)

---

8. Abbott-Smith, *A Manual Greek Lexicon*, 184.

Since Jesus as the *māšiah* was the ideal Davidic king, not only was the Davidic kingship enthroned through him, but God's kingdom too had come. This was the way the good news was "the good news of the kingdom" (see e.g. Matt 4:23; 24:14; Luke 8:1). Jesus advanced the kingdom of God, as taught in the parable of the sower amongst those who believed in the good news (Matt 13:18–23; Mark 4:13–20; Luke 8:11–15). This was demonstrated by their freedom from Satan and evil spirits by the exorcism of both (Matt 12:28; Luke 13:32), by their healing and being made whole, by their cleansing of leprosy, and by raising the dead (see Mark 1:32–34; 3:7–11; Matt 4:23; 8:16; 11:4–5; Luke 7:21–22; 13:32). In contrast, unbelief hindered his advance of the kingdom so that no demonstration of the kingdom of God was experienced by unbelievers: "And he did not do many deeds of power there, because of their unbelief" (Matt 13:58; Mark 6:5–6).

Jesus, then, as the pastor of Israel, fulfilled his pastoral ministry of giving the word of God to God's people by proclaiming the word of God – God's timely word that the kingdom of God had arrived with his coming as the *māšiah*.

Teaching the word of God
We now consider Jesus's teaching by first examining Matthew and Mark's account. Although the narrator of Matthew's gospel rarely refers directly to Jesus's addresses as *didaskōn* (teachings), the five sets of "sayings" (*logous*) in Matthew that we earlier mentioned are equated to *didaskōn* in the gospel itself: "Now when Jesus had finished saying (*logous*) these things, the crowds were astounded at his teaching (*didaskōn*)" (Matt 7:28). Consequently, not only was teaching the hallmark of Jesus's pastoral ministry but also the content of the Gospel of Matthew.

Matthew's narration of Jesus's extensive teaching is replicated (albeit differently) in Mark. Mark's gospel highlights that it was Jesus's custom to teach: "And crowds again gathered around him; and, as was his custom, he again taught them" (Mark 10:1). More than any of the other Gospels, Mark directly shows that Jesus's ministry was characterized by his place-to-place teaching. So, in Mark's gospel, we read that Jesus taught in the synagogue (Mark 1:21; 6:2), beside the sea (Mark 2:13), by the lake (Mark 4:1), and in the temple (Mark 11:17; 12:35–40).

Turning our attention to Luke and John, it is reported by the narrators that Jesus taught three times in Luke and two times in John. In Luke Jesus taught on a Sabbath (Luke 4:31), once from a boat in the lake of Gennesaret (Luke 5:3), and on his way to Jerusalem (Luke 13:22). In John, he taught during the Feast of Tabernacles (7:14), and in the temple (John 8:2).

Crucially, we learn from John's gospel that Jesus himself specifically testified that teaching occupied him: "Jesus answered, 'I have always taught in synagogues and in the temple, where all the Jews come together'" (John 18:20). But how could this be the case against few references of Jesus teaching (*didaskōn*) that are reported in Luke and John? It is when we go by what *didaskōn* meant within the Jewish religious context during the time of Jesus that we come to understand the full extent that both Gospels depict Jesus's toil as primarily teaching. We turn to this in what follows, and in so doing, simultaneously show that in the Gospels Jesus as the pastor of Israel fulfilled his pastoral ministry of giving the word of God to the people of Israel chiefly through teaching the word.

In the Gospels we see that Jesus was referred to as "rabbi" (*rabbi* – Mark 9:5; 11:21; 14:45; Matt 26:25, 49; John 1:38, 49; 4:31) which was the Aramaic word for *didaskalon* (teacher) in Greek (see e.g. Mark 4:38; 9:17; 10:17; Matt 12:38; 17:24; 19:16; Luke 7:40; 9:38; 19:39; John 8:4; 11:28; 13:13–14). The synonymous use of these two words for teacher in the Gospels is captured in John where Nicodemus referred to Jesus using both words in the same sentence; "Rabbi, we know that you are a teacher who has come from God" (John 3:2).

However, Jesus was not the only one referred to as *rabbi* in the Gospels; scribes and Pharisees were also referred to as *rabbi* (Matt 23:7; John 3:10) because they were, like Jesus, teachers. In comparison however Jesus was seen to have taught with authority: "They were astounded at his teaching, for he taught them as one having authority, and not as the scribes" (Mark 1:22; Matt 7:29). Thus, in understanding the particular kind of teaching the scribes and Pharisees undertook, we shall appreciate that Jesus as the shepherd of Israel fulfilled his pastoral ministry of delivering God's word through teaching it to God's people.

From the Gospels we learn that the scribes and Pharisees taught the word of God that was preserved in the Scriptures – the writings (*graphai*) that were available to them. They did so by explaining or clarifying them for their listeners and instructing them on ways to follow them in their daily living. According to Matthew's gospel, Jesus recognized that the scribes and Pharisees taught God's people the word of the Lord, in this case the law, thereby exercising the functions which Moses had (through whom they received the law). This is why he instructed their listeners to obey them but not follow their deeds:

> Then Jesus said to the crowds and to his disciples, "The scribes and the Pharisees sit on Moses' seat; therefore, do whatever they teach you and follow it; but do not do as they do, for they do not

practice what they do, for they do not practice what they teach. (Matt 23:1–3)

It is with this kind of teaching that Jesus was involved; he too taught the word of God. Matthew's gospel gives the most direct examples of Jesus doing so, particularly in the first set of Jesus's teaching (Matt 5:1–7:28) where he quoted the Scriptures, interpreted them, and clarified their application. But there are other specific instances in the Gospels which point to Jesus's teaching as of the scribal and Pharisaic kind. Taking three examples from Mark, he taught the Scriptures on matters of purity (Mark 7:1–9); taught them Scriptures about God's house when he drove out traders from it: "and he would not allow anyone to carry anything through the temple; and was teaching them and saying, 'Is it not written . . .'" (Mark 11:16–19). He also taught on Psalm 100:1 concerning his kingship (Mark 12:35–37).

Jesus's teaching in synagogues (see e.g. Matt 4:23; 9:35; 13:54; Mark 1:21; 6:2; Luke 4:15; 6:6; 13:10; John 6:59; 18:20) further demonstrates that he delivered God's word to God's people by teaching it. It was in synagogues, as we witness in Luke 4:16–17, that the Scriptures were read and interpreted. As a point in fact, the seat of Moses, upon which Jesus mentioned the scribes and Pharisees sat (Matt 23:2), was later a physical seat in synagogues so that those who sat on them would teach the Scriptures to those who had gathered.[9] Since the Gospels mention that Jesus taught in the synagogues, it follows that his teaching was the word of God as read out from the Scriptures.

But the word of God which Jesus taught was, unlike the scribal and Pharisaic one, not limited to the interpretation and application of the Scriptures. As the shepherd of Israel, Jesus specifically proclaimed to the Israelites, as we pointed out earlier, God's timely word that his kingdom had dawned upon them. As a consequence, Jesus spoke about the meaning of this fulfilment to those who believed in him by teaching about the kingdom (Acts 1:3) as the following examples illustrate. He taught that humility (e.g. Matt 18:1–4; Mark 9:33–35; Luke 9:46–48), and service (e.g. Mark 10:35–45; Matt 20:20–28; 25:31–46; John 13:5–15) were cardinal virtues of the kingdom. He taught that the kingdom spread through healing and exorcism (Matt 12:22–32), as it was spiritual in nature (John 18:36). He taught of its inconspicuous beginnings and growth but eventual universal scale (e.g. Matt 13:31–32; Mark 4:30–32). He taught about its incomparable value (Matt 13:44–45). He taught that people

---

9. E. L. Sukenik, *Ancient Synagogues in Palestine and Greece* (London: Oxford University Press, 1934), 57–61.

entered it through faith (e.g. Matt 4:17; Mark 1:15; Luke 8:11–15; John 3:1–15), and repentance (e.g. Matt 4:17; Mark 1:15) for which reason he warned against non-repentance (e.g. Matt 12:38–42; 21:28–32; Luke 13:1–9) and pointed out the joy that repentance brought (Luke 15:3–10).

In addition, as a prophet who was also God's Son, Jesus's words were the word of God. As alluded to earlier, this is most clear in John's gospel where the narrator reveals that Jesus on several occasions let it be known that his words were actually the word of God (John 3:34; 7:16–17; 8:28; 12:49; 17:8). As we mentioned, this was the way the divine *logos* was concretely manifest. Jesus therefore taught God's word that was not contained in the Scriptures the people had. His words were the words of God; thus the command to his disciples to listen to him: "This is my Son, the beloved; listen to him!" (Mark 9:7). Subsequently, his words would be preserved orally and later in writing and be taught as the word of God (more on this later).

The argument so far demonstrates that as the pastor of Israel, teaching the word of God was the primary way that Jesus fulfilled the pastoral ministry of giving God's word to his people. To be called *rabbi* or *didaskalon* was an indication that teaching characterized his work.

4. Primary Activities of the Pastoral Ministry in the Early Church
Preaching and teaching predominated in the Apostles' pastoral ministry

The apostles numbered twelve to symbolize that they were the leaders of Israel to correspond to the number of their tribes. From the Gospels we learn that Jesus, as the pastor of Israel, did not singularly fulfil the pastoral ministry of giving God's word to God's people but did so with the twelve apostles because he chose them to shepherd Israel alongside him. Thus, the twelve apostles as pastors of Israel (and later Gentiles too) also fulfilled the pastoral ministry of giving God's word to God's people through preaching and teaching. Initially Jesus fulfilled with them the pastoral ministry of giving the Israelites God's word when he directed them to go into Galilee to preach the word: "He appointed the twelve – designating them apostles – that they might be with him, and that he might send them out to preach" (Mark 3:14 NIV; see also Matt 10:7; Luke 9:2).

After the ascension Jesus left them behind to carry on with this pastoral ministry by commanding them specifically to preach the word, but this time, everywhere in the world. If we are able to regard Mark 16:15 as part of primitive text as some have argued we should,[10] Jesus commanded the apostles to go into all the world and preach the good news. The same is implied in Luke because the preaching that would begin in Jerusalem, which Jesus mentioned (Luke 24:47) would be carried out by the apostles as his witnesses (Luke 24:48; Acts 1:8). In Acts, Peter refers to this command which Jesus gave as the reason for his preaching to Cornelius and his household (Acts 10:42).

We also find the command to the apostles to fulfil the pastoral ministry of giving God's word to God's people in Matthew through teaching (*didaskōn*) it: "Go therefore and make disciples of all nations . . . teaching them to obey everything that I have commanded you" (Matt 28:19–20). The apostles' pastoral ministry of teaching God's word, as pastors of Jews and Gentiles, was backed by the authority which Jesus gave them: "Truly I tell you, whatever you bind on earth will be bound in heaven, and whatever you loose on earth will be loosened in heaven (Matt 18:18). Such was the magnitude of the authority of their pastoral ministry that in the words of Patrick Harling, "The disciples of Matthew . . . are the ones who possess this full authority to bring about God's will here in earth,"[11] by teaching no less than God's word.

In John, the command to the apostles to give God's word after Jesus's physical departure is seen in Jesus's command to Peter to feed his sheep (John 20:15–17). If we recall our understanding of the shepherd-sheep metaphor where feeding of sheep was analogous to giving God's people his word, Jesus was, in concrete terms, commanding Peter to give God's people his word. However, this command was not given solely to Peter but to the twelve apostles whom Peter, as their leader, represented.

According to the New Testament, Paul was an apostle alongside the Twelve as indicated in the parallels between himself and the apostles. Just as Jesus had appeared to the disciples after his resurrection, he also appeared to Paul (1 Cor 15:8–9; see also 1 Cor 9:1). Moreover, and, perhaps more importantly, just as Jesus had commissioned the apostles to fulfil the pastoral ministry of giving God's word through preaching and teaching, he also sent him to do so amongst the Gentiles (Acts 9:15–16; Acts 22:21). Paul himself testified to this commission to the Galatians – "But when God . . . was pleased to reveal his Son in me, so that I might preach him amongst the Gentiles" (Gal 1:15–16 NIV) – as well as to the Corinthians (1 Cor 1:17). He also talked of his labours to preach the

---

10. See N. C. Croy, *The Mutilation of Mark's Gospel* (Nashville: Abingdon Press, 2003).

11. Patrick J. Hartin, "Disciples as authorities within Matthew's Christian-Jewish community," *Neot* 32, no. 2 (1998): 389–404, 398.

gospel directly as a commission (1 Cor 9:17). For this reason, Paul alongside the Twelve was designated as Jesus's witness (Acts 22:15; see also Acts 20:24).

The book of Acts shows that the apostles as pastors of Jews and Gentiles fulfilled their pastoral ministry of giving God's word to God's people through their preaching and teaching. The five speeches in Acts (following Padilla's classification)[12] provide ample evidence of apostolic preaching and teaching. In the first speech, Peter preached and taught on the day when the Spirit of God descended on the apostles (Acts 2:1–41). In the third speech, he also preached to the household of Cornelius (Acts 10:34–48). In the fourth speech, Paul preached and taught in Athens (Acts 17:16–31), while in the fifth speech, he preached before King Agrippa (Acts 26:1–32).

Besides the apostles' preaching and teaching contained in their speeches, we have evidence of their teaching and preaching in other sections of Acts' narrative. They all preached and taught for some time "every day in the temple and at home" (Acts 5:42). Peter and John preached and taught with John in Solomon's Portico (Acts 3:11). They also are said to have preached the good news in many villages of the Samaritans (Acts 8:25). What is more, they themselves declared their commitment to preaching the word when other leadership responsibilities came calling: "And the twelve summoned the body of the disciples and said, 'It is not right that we should give up preaching the word of God to serve tables'" (Acts 6:2). Their devotion to the word is corroborated by their description as "servants (*hupēretai*) of the word" (Luke 1:2).

In other instances of apostolic preaching and teaching in Acts, Paul the apostle is said to have preached with John in the synagogues of Salamis and the island of Paphos (Acts 13:5–6). He himself preached on several occasions in Perga; first on the Sabbath day in a synagogue there (Acts 13:16–48), and then in Perga generally (Acts 14:24). He also taught in the synagogue of Jews in Thessalonica (Acts 17:2), preached in Beroea (Acts 17:13) and in various places in Athens (Acts 17:18). He also preached and taught under house arrest in Rome (Acts 28:30–31). Paul himself in his farewell to the Ephesian *presbuteroi* (elders) mentions that he was continually preaching and teaching them (Acts 20:20, 25, 27). Elsewhere, Paul states that he taught "everywhere and in every church" (1 Cor 4:17).

---

12. Osvaldo Padilla, *The Acts of the Apostles: Interpretation, History and Theology* (London: Apollos, 2016).

Teachers, prophets, and elders-bishops; apostles' designations for pastoral ministry

Viewed from a different perspective, the apostles' designations also underline that they fulfilled their pastoral ministry of giving God's people his word through preaching and teaching. In other words, their designations defined their pastoral ministry. First was their designation as preachers and as teachers. Paul referred to himself a preacher and a teacher of the word. According to his pastoral letters to Timothy, Paul pointed out twice that besides his appointment to be an apostle, he was also appointed to be a preacher and teacher of the good news: "For this I was appointed a preacher and apostle (I am telling the truth and not lying) and a teacher" (1 Tim 2:7 ESV; see also 2 Tim 1:11). He also singled out preaching as a task with which God had entrusted him (Eph 3:8; Titus 1:3).

Second was their designation as prophets. We come across this designation in the Epistle to the Ephesians which, in articulating the foundational nature of the ministry of the apostles, refers to them in a double fashion as "apostles and prophets" (Eph 2:20), and then as "holy apostles and prophets" of Jesus (Eph 3:5). What makes us view these references to prophets here to be strictly references to the apostles and not to other prophets or persons, is the content of the revelation: the mystery of Christ. This mystery, as the verses make clear, was revealed exclusively to Jesus's apostles, of which Paul was one, by the Lord himself and whose content they were commissioned to preach and teach:

> For surely you have heard of the commission of God's grace that was given me for you, and how the mystery was made known to me by revelation, as I wrote above in a few words, a reading which will enable you to perceive my understanding of the mystery of Christ. In the former generations this mystery was not made known to humankind, as it has now been revealed to his holy apostles and prophets by the Spirit. (Eph 3:2–5)

We could add here a reference from Revelation. It appears that John the apostle, the seer in the apocalypse, is designated together with the other apostles as a prophet: "I am your fellow servant with you and your brothers the prophets" (Rev 22:9 NEB).

We also have another instance of an apostle designated as a prophet in Paul albeit in association with his designation as a teacher. Together with four others persons in prayers and fasting in Antioch, Paul was designated as prophet and teacher:

> Now in the church at Antioch there were prophets and teachers (*prophētai kai didaskaloi*): Barnabas, Simeon, who was called Niger, Lucius of Cyrene, Manean a member of the court of Herod the ruler, and Saul. While they were worshipping the Lord and fasting . . . (Acts 13:1–2)

In referring to the five jointly as "prophets and teachers," Luke does not tell us who amongst them were *prophētai* and who were *didaskaloi*. The reason for this twin reference of the five is most likely that distinguishing who were the prophets and who were the teachers was not of any fundamental importance because the two were not distinct categories or functions but rather designations of persons with the same role which was the pastoral ministry of giving the word of God. This is akin to referring to a group of teachers in a university jointly as senior lecturers and lecturers without much ado since both play the same role of teaching.

That said however, there is decisive evidence in the New Testament that amongst persons fulfilling the pastoral ministry of giving the word of God by proclaiming and teaching the Scriptures were those who, additionally, also gave, like the prophets in the Old Testament, what we termed God's timely word. If we may remind ourselves, we showed that prophets in the Old Testament did not just proclaim the law and warn about disobeying it, but gave the word of God in specific ways that were related to peoples' circumstances, thoughts and emotions. Consequently, their word would tell God's people what they needed to do or not do, as well as revealing to them what God was doing or was going to do. Their word as God's word was therefore revelatory; it was God's word at that specific time for his people – God's timely word. Agabus, who was referred to as a prophet, demonstrates that prophets after the advent and physical departure of Jesus also gave God's timely word. Being a prophet, he gave God's timely word about an impending famine in the world, and about the arrest of Paul by his fellow Jews:

> At that time prophets came down from Jerusalem to Antioch. One of them named Agabus stood up and predicted by the Spirit that there would be a severe famine over the world, and this took place during the reign of Claudius. (Acts 11:27–28)

> While we were staying there for several days, a prophet named Agabus came down from Judea. He came to us and took Paul's belt, bound his own feet and hands with it, and said, "Thus says the Holy Spirit, 'This is the way the Jews in Jerusalem will bind the

man who owns this belt and will hand him over to the Gentiles.'" (Acts 21:10–11)

Thus the apostles, by being also referred to as prophets, fulfilled the pastoral ministry of giving God's word both by preaching and teaching the Scriptures, and by giving God's timely word. This outlook is epitomized in Paul who not only, as we have already pointed out, elsewhere referred to himself as a teacher (1 Tim 2:7; 2 Tim 1:11), but also intimated that he was a prophet by giving God's timely word: "Anyone who claims to be a prophet, or to have spiritual powers, must acknowledge that what I am writing to you is a command of the Lord" (1 Cor 14:37).

The third and last designation of apostles which showed that as pastors of both Jews and Gentiles they were fulfilling their pastoral ministry of giving God's people his word through preaching and teaching, was their designations as "elders" (*presbuteroi*). According to the first Epistle of Peter, Peter addressed elders as fellow elders (*sumpresbuteroi*) because he was a *presbuteros* himself: "And now I appeal to the elders of your community, as a fellow-elder" (1 Pet 5:1 GNB). Peter exhorted the elders specifically to give oversight (*episkopountes*) willingly and by example to God's flock as he himself must have been doing. In consequence, they were also bishops (*episkopoi*) or, strictly speaking, elders-bishops (*presbuteroi-episkopoi* from here on).

The oversight/supervision (*episkopē*) as *episkopoi*, that was alluded to in Peter's exhortation, is that of pastors: the pastoral ministry of giving God's word by preaching and teaching. The exemplary lives of elders-bishops by which they were to "tend the flock" presumed their teaching of the word upon which they had modelled their lives. It should not then be taken as incidental that Peter invoked Scripture to point out that Judas had to be replaced so that another apostle would take over his oversight/supervision (*episkopēv*), but rather a revelation of the apostles' pastoral ministry:

> For it is written in the book of Psalms,
>
> "Let his homestead become desolate,
> and let there be no one to love in it":
>
> and
>
> "Let another take his position of overseer." (Acts 1:20)

Since an *episkopē* (an oversight) was given by an *episkopos* (an overseer), there could be no *episkopē* without an *episkopos*. Consequently, all the apostles were elder-bishops as is clarified in this first Epistle of Peter. This pastoral ministry of preaching and teaching that defined their oversight over God's flock mirrored (but to a lesser extent) that of Jesus since, in this context of Peter's exhortation, he was the chief elder-bishop (1 Pet 5:4).

Teaching and preaching by other prophets, teachers, and elders-bishops

In Acts as well as in some other books of the New Testament, we learn that the pastoral ministry of giving God's word was not exclusive to the apostles. The pastoral ministry that Jesus carried out as the pastor of Israel was not just left to his apostles, but was also conducted by others, which meant that there were other pastors besides the apostles. Alongside the apostles and independent of them, these pastors gave the word by preaching and teaching. We have a series of examples here. Stephen, whom the apostles appointed a deacon, preached (albeit in a short-lived manner) to the Jews (Acts 7:2–53). Philip, the other deacon, also preached and taught the word (Acts 8:4–8, 26–40). Barnabas preached alongside Paul in the synagogue in Salamis (Acts 13:4–5), and also in the Island of Paphos (Acts 13:12). Silas and Timothy preached and taught alongside Paul in Macedonia (Acts 16:10). In Lystra and Derbe, Barnabas preached alongside Paul (Acts 14:1, 7, 15), as he did in Antioch (15:35). We therefore have in the New Testament non-apostolic prophets, *presbuteroi-episkopoi*, and teachers (whom we shall refer to as the apostles' "non-apostolic counterparts") as we show below.

There are a number of non-apostolic prophets both specific and undefined mentioned in the New Testament which demonstrates that alongside the apostles were other pastors who, in addition to preaching and teaching the word, also gave God's timely word. We pointed out that Barnabas, Simeon Niger, and Lucius were designated together with Paul as prophets, albeit in association with their designation as teachers (Acts 13:1). Consequently, we understand that these four, just like Paul, proclaimed and taught Scripture, but also, in addition, gave God's timely word. Besides these four is the mention of Judas and Silas (Acts 15:32), and a number of prophets in Jerusalem (Acts 11:27) and in the church at Corinth (1 Cor 14:29–32, 37). We also have, as we have pointed out already, a prophet called Agabus, whose operations as described in Acts pointed to why some amongst those fulfilling the pastoral ministry of giving God's word were referred to as prophets. There is also mention of an indefinite number of prophets in Rome whom Paul encouraged to serve believers (Rom 12:4) in line with their prophetic gift (as demonstrated in Agabus), through prophecy (*prophēteian*):

> We have gifts that differ according to the grace given to us: prophecy, in proportion to faith, ministry in ministering; the teacher, in teaching; the exhorter, in exhortation; the giver, in generosity; the leader, in diligence; the compassionate, in cheerfulness. (Rom 12:6–8; see also Acts 15:30–32 on exhortation by prophets Judas and Silas)

As a last instance of non-apostolic prophets in the New Testament, there must have been prophets amongst the audience of Peter's first Epistle even if they are not mentioned directly. Encouraging speakers – "any who speaks" (*tis lalei*) – to do so as if they were speaking the "oracles of God," *logia Thiou*, presupposed that those speakers were prophets:

> As each has received a gift, employ it for one another, as good stewards of God's varied grace: whoever speaks, as one who utters *oracles of God*; whoever renders service, as one who renders it by the strength which God supplies. (1 Pet 4:10–11 RSV, my emphasis)

This must have been the case because *logia Thiou* were prophecies, which only prophets could give, and not general proclamations or teaching of the word of God. Being the very words of God, *logia Thiou* could only be given by those who had some revelation from God or were inspired by his Spirit, which were the means by which prophets were able to give God's timely word.

As for non-apostolic *presbuteroi-episkopoi*, elders were appointed in the churches of Lystria and Iconium in the province of Lycaonia, and Antioch of the province of Pisidia (Acts 14:23). There were elders too in Jerusalem who, revealingly, were paired with the apostles (Acts 15:2–6; Acts 15:22–23; Acts 16:4), and reference is made of Paul meeting all the elders when he went to Jerusalem at the end of his third missionary journey (Acts 21:18). In Miletus, Paul addressed the elders in the church of Ephesus (Acts 20:17–18).

As we have already pointed out in 1 Peter, the oversight/supervision (*episkopē*) which the elders provided was preaching and teaching God's word. This is confirmed in the pastoral letter to Titus in the same way as in 1 Peter. The elders were also bishops, as demonstrated in the synonymity between the two designations whereby instructions given to elders in one sentence continue to be given to them in the next, but then as bishops. And here too the *episkopē* of the *episkopoi* was the pastoral ministry of preaching and teaching the word:

> ... and should *appoint elders* in every town as I directed you: someone who is blameless, married only once ... *For a bishop*, as

Preaching and Teaching the Word: the Primary Activities in Pastoral Ministry

> God's steward, must be blameless . . . He must have a firm grasp of the word that is trustworthy in accordance with the teaching, so that he may be able to preach with sound doctrine and to refute those who contradict it. (Titus 1:5–9, my emphasis)

Although not designated as such, it would appear that Timothy and Titus were, alongside the apostles, *presbuteroi-episkopoi*, because of the emphasis on teaching in the various instructions that were given to them:

> These are the things you must insist on and teach. (1 Tim 4:11)
>
> Attend to the public reading of Scripture, to preaching, to teaching. (1 Tim 4:13 RSV)
>
> Pay close attention to yourself and to your teaching. (1 Tim 4:16)
>
> Do your best to present yourself to God as one approved by him, a worker who had no need to be ashamed, rightly explaining the word of truth. (2 Tim 2:15)
>
> And the Lord's servant must not be quarrelsome but kindly to everyone, an apt teacher. (2 Tim 2:24)
>
> I give you this charge: preach the word (2 Tim 4:1–2a NIV)
>
> Reprove, rebuke, and exhort, with complete patience and teaching. (2 Tim 4:2b ESV)
>
> But as for you, teach what is consistent with sound doctrine. (Titus 2:1)
>
> Show yourself in all respects a model of good works, and in your teaching show integrity. (Titus 2:7)
>
> Teach these things and use your full authority as you encourage. (Titus 2:15 GNB)

Coming to non-apostolic teachers, we have a series of references to such teachers in the New Testament. Barnabas, Simeon Niger, and Lucius were designated, again, with Paul as teachers too (Acts 13:1). Apollos together with Priscilla and Aquila seemed to have been teachers for they are highlighted in the narrative as having knowledge of the word on which basis they taught it (Acts 18:24–28). There were teachers in the church at Corinth (1 Cor 12:29). We had teachers in the church in Galatia whom Paul was aware of in advising the believers there to share good things with them: "Those who are taught the word must share in all good things with their teacher" (Gal 6:6).

James, traditionally identified to be the brother of Jesus, was himself a teacher. But he was aware of other teachers amongst the believers to whom he addressed his Epistle, and felt compelled to warn the rest not to desire to become teachers in view of their responsibilities and thus judgement: "Not many of you should become teachers, my brothers and sisters, for you know that we who teach will be judged with greater strictness" (Jas 3:1). Last in our series of references to non-apostolic teachers are *presbuteroi-episkopoi*. The contrast between Timothy as a *presbuteros-episkopos* and false teachers (2 Tim 4:1–4) made sense because Timothy was, unlike them, a true teacher. For this reason, *presbuteroi-episkopoi* were also teachers who deserved greater honour than other leaders (1 Tim 5:17–18).

Teaching and preaching by evangelists

We now turn to look at "evangelist" as another designation of non-apostolic pastors in the New Testament. We look at the designation on its own for three reasons. Firstly, unlike the pastoral designations of the apostles as teacher, prophet, and *presbuteros-episkopos*, this one is not used to refer to them. Secondly, of the three mentions of the designation we find in the New Testament, only once is it used to refer to a specific person. Lastly, it is undefined and not demonstrated, thus making its meaning vague.

Philip is the person in the New Testament specifically referred to as an "evangelist," *euangelistēs*: "The next day we left and came to Caesarea; and we went into the house of Philip the evangelist (*tou euangelistou*)" (Acts 21:8). For this reason he is our only concrete point of reference of an *euangelistēs* in apostolic times. So we may ask here, what it is that we know about Philip that may help us to understand who an evangelist was. We know, as we have already discussed, that Philip preached and taught the word:

> Now, those who were scattered went from place to place, proclaiming the word. Philip went down to the city of Samaria and proclaimed the Messiah to them. The crowds with one accord listened eagerly to what was said by Philip, hearing and seeing the signs he did. (Acts 8:4–6; see also Acts 8:26–40)

He therefore fulfilled the pastoral ministry of preaching and teaching. Consequently, whatever may be said of the evangelists in apostolic times, they were pastors alongside those non-apostolic pastors who were referred to as teachers, prophets and elders-bishops.

In 2 Timothy 4:5, Paul instructed Timothy to do the work of an *euangelistēs*: "As for you, always be sober-minded, endure suffering, do the work of an evangelist, fulfill your ministry." It would be odd for Paul to have instructed Timothy to do that work if the work of an *euangelistēs* was unknown. We must then seek to determine what made some pastors be referred to as evangelists.

The place to look for an understanding of an evangelist in the New Testament is by looking at what that the common noun implies the person did, as communicated in the verb directly related to it and its cognate *euangelion* (which means "good news"). The verb that is directly derived from *euangelistēs* and *euangelion* is *euangelizomai*, which is translated variously as "announce the good news," "bring good news," or "proclaim the gospel." The first thing we must note is that the verb has to do with preaching or proclaiming, which signifies that it was an activity they undertook as pastors. But more importantly, it pinpoints the content of what was proclaimed, which is the good news.

As we discussed previously, the good news which Jesus proclaimed was about the kingdom of God. We shall demonstrate later in this chapter when we look at the content of preaching and teaching, that after his ascension, the good news would include him on account of his role in ushering in, expanding, and establishing that kingdom. Now according to the New Testament, Jesus, the apostles and their non-apostolic counterparts preached the good news. Jesus is said to have preached the good news to the poor (Matt 11:5), in towns (Luke 4:43), in cities and villages (Luke 8:1), and even in the temple (Luke 20:1). Paul also preached the good news in Athens (Acts 17:18), Corinth (1 Cor 15:1), Galatia (Gal 1:11) and other places in his missionary journeys. Barnabas (with Paul) also preached in Lystra and Derbe (Acts 14:7, 15, 21), and in Antioch (Acts 15:35). Silas and Timothy (together with Paul) preached the gospel (Acts 16:10). Philip being himself our concrete reference of an evangelist preached the good news to a city in Samaria (Acts 8:12), to the Ethiopian eunuch (Acts 8:35), and in various towns on his way to Caesarea (Acts 8:40).

An evangelist, then, according to the New Testament was one who preached the good news. But Paul, Silas, Barnabas, and Timothy who preached the good news were not referred to as evangelists. Indeed, concerning Timothy, as we noted, Paul urged him to take on the role of an evangelist (2 Tim 4:5) presumably because he would not have been considered to be one. Preaching the good news by pastors in apostolic times did not therefore automatically make them evangelists. It is most likely that pastors who were called evangelists must have had their preaching visibly defined by their preaching of the gospel. Consequently, pastors would have been called evangelists because their preaching was very often about the good news. In their preaching, the preaching of the good news was so frequent that they became inevitably associated with it to the extent that they were called *euangelistēs* – preachers of the good news. In this sense, we could say that Timothy could do the work of an evangelist as instructed, by frequently preaching the good news as evangelists did, even if not to the same extent (otherwise he would himself become an evangelist which Paul was not asking him to become).

From this perspective, it makes sense that evangelists were grouped together with teachers and prophets in Ephesians 4:11, which we turn to before concluding with a look at the purpose for preaching and teaching the word. Ephesians 4:11 is a text worthy of a study on its own for two reasons. The first is that it is a verse which is commonly referred to in conversations and discussions about ministry. The second, and more fundamental, is that it is the only text in the New Testament where the designations of all those who fulfilled the pastoral ministry of preaching and teaching, except for elders-bishops, are placed together. Understanding this text therefore is crucial in our study of ministry in biblical perspective.

Apostles, prophets, evangelists, and shepherd-teachers in Ephesians 4:11

> And he gave the apostles, the prophets, the evangelists, the shepherds and teachers, to equip the saints for the work of ministry, for building up the body of Christ.... (Eph 4:11–12 ESV)

As the preceding verses of this chapter show, before making this revelation, Paul had pointed out that Christ Jesus had given gifts (Eph 4:7). He related this to YHWH giving gifts to his people as celebrated and recalled in Psalm 68.[13] In that psalm, YHWH was praised as a victorious king over his enemies, and over other kings and their armies. Subsequent to his victory, he was pictured making his processional ascent to his abode the temple with captives in his wake and receiving gifts from people (Ps 68:15–18). Thus, like YHWH, Jesus Christ is revealed as the cosmic king who upon his victorious ascension to his throne at God's right hand (Eph 2:20) "far above all the heavens" (Eph 4:10) distributed gifts:

---

13. Although only Psalm 68:18 is apparently quoted, it is actually the whole psalm that is applied to Christ, as discussed by Gombis. It would be very difficult to account for Psalm 68:18's paraphrasing whereby "receives" (*elabes*) is replaced by "gives" (*edōken*), and its ensuing application to Christ, unless the whole psalm was in view. See Timothy G. Gombis, "Cosmic Lordship and Divine Gift-Giving: Psalm 68 in Ephesian 4:8," *Novum Testamentum* 47.4 (2005): 367–380.

> Therefore it is said,
> When he ascended on high he led a host of captives,
> and he gave gifts to men. (Eph 4:8 ESV)

However, in an unprecedented, even extraordinary, way, Paul revealed in Ephesians 4:11 that the gifts Christ Jesus gave were people, or more precisely a group of people, namely, apostles, prophets, evangelists, and "teaching shepherds."

Common to all those in this group that is the gift ("group gift" from here on) of Christ, as demonstrated in our NT study, was their role of preaching and teaching the word in fulfilment of their pastoral responsibility to give God's word to his people (Carson appropriately calls their ministry "word-ministries").[14] Persons in this group gift were in essence gifted by Christ with the ability to give the word of God to God's people. In other words this is a group of people who, having being chosen to be shepherds of God's people, were endowed with the pastoral gift of preaching and teaching thereby becoming Christ's gift to the church. Preaching and teaching God's word must, therefore, have been the means by which the grace (*charis*) Paul mentioned was mediated to every believer according to Christ's measure: "But each of us was given grace according to the measure of Christ's gift" (Eph 4:7).

Ephesians 4:12–16 clarifies preaching and teaching as the means of grace to believers by emphasizing the place of knowledge in the growth of believers. Knowledge for growth is envisaged both in terms of its instrumentality in bringing about that growth, and its full acquisition as the end point of the growth. Specifically, the purpose of Christ's group gift was for the growth of believers by means of the knowledge which they would acquire through the preaching and teaching of the word by members of this group gift. That word is talked of in the Epistle as truth spoken (*alētheuontes* – Eph 4:15), the knowledge of which would get rid of ignorance that would make God's people vulnerable to erroneous teachings peddled craftily by those whose agenda is to deceive them. Ultimately, that truth would also bring them to maturity – the same knowledge as that of Jesus the Son of God:

> To equip the saints for the work of ministry, for the building up of the body of Christ, until all of us come to the unity of the faith and of the knowledge of the Son of God, to maturity, to the measure of the full stature of Christ. We must no longer be children, tossed to and fro and blown about by every wind of doctrine, by people's trickery, by their craftiness in deceitful scheming. But speaking

---

14. D. A. Carson, "Do the Work of an Evangelist," *Them* 39, no. 1 (2014): 1–4, 3.

the truth in love, we must grow up in every way into him who is the head, into Christ. (Eph 4:12–16)

The revelation of Christ's group gift upon his ascension for the sake of knowledge for growth and maturity through the word coheres with the witness of the New Testament elsewhere where we learn of Jesus's commissioning of the twelve apostles. They carried out their commission to teach and preach soon after Jesus's ascension back to God to sit at his right hand. The day of Pentecost can be viewed as the day they were gifted to preach and teach by the enabling power of the Spirit sent by God at Christ's behest (John 14:16–17; 15:26). Indeed they were told not to begin preaching and teaching but to wait until the promised Holy Spirit was sent (Acts 1:4–5, 8). With the coming of the Spirit, they were gifted to preach and teach for the growth of every believer.

Although those in this group gift were preachers and teachers of the word, they are referred to in four different ways. These different references for pastors pointed to some distinctions amongst them which all revolved around preaching and teaching the word, the primary activity of pastoral ministry which they all fulfilled as pastors. However these differences can only be spoken of in very general terms.

From our discussion, we know that those referred to as apostles were the Twelve who had been with Jesus and whom he specially commissioned to preach and teach. As for prophets and evangelists, we pointed out that the former were pastors who gave God's timely word, while the latter were pastors who in conspicuous ways preached the gospel frequently in their preaching of the word.

Before appreciating pastors referred to as "the shepherds and teachers," we must first look more closely at what that reference could have meant. We should start by noting in Ephesians 4:11 that while all the other references have a definite article *tous*, it only appears before shepherds, but not before teachers thus: *kai autos edōke tous men apostolous, tous de prophētas, tous de euangelistas, tous de poimenas kai didaskalous*. Our preferred translation of the verse from ESV (also TNIV) which we quoted above captures this well by rendering a most literal translation: "He gave the apostles, the prophets, the evangelists, and the shepherds and teachers." Most versions substitute "some" for the definite article, and so read, "some to be apostles, some to be prophets . . . ," thus missing out on the implication of the definite article which is that it links shepherds and teachers, thereby making the two one set of individuals known as "shepherds and teachers." As Barth[15] pointed out, this reference could then be translated concretely to read; "teaching shepherds," or "shepherding teachers" to communicate what was intended: one set of pastors. This is the reason why we ourselves have accordingly rendered it as "teaching shepherds."

However, a question that has to do with *poimenas* – which literally means "shepherds" but has been translated as "pastors" in most English versions of the Bible (see NRSV, NASB, TNIV, and GNB) – remains. We have avoided quoting this verse from versions that translate it as "pastors" in order to limit the reading of common notions of pastors into this compound reference. *Poimēn*, "shepherd," is not used in the New Testament to refer to apostolic and non-apostolic pastors. It is used, but in two instances only, to refer to Jesus as the great shepherd (Heb 13:20) and as the chief shepherd (1 Pet 5:4). And in the gospel narratives Jesus referred to himself once as the good shepherd (John 10:11). We therefore have no concrete reference to an apostolic or non-apostolic pastor as a *poimen* from whom we can work out what distinguished pastors who were called "shepherds." In addition, since *poimēn* is a noun metaphor we cannot simply study the word in the abstract, as we can when looking at a verb metaphor, without considering the context from which it is drawn, to help us find out what a pastor who was a shepherd did.

This is the reason why in our study we have rooted our understanding of Jesus as a shepherd in the Old Testament's shepherding responsibilities of priests and prophets who were non-executive human shepherds of Israel. Our study has resulted in our understanding of preaching and teaching the word of God as a primary activity of human shepherds: priests and prophets in the Old Testament and accordingly Jesus, the apostles and their non-apostolic counterparts in the New Testament. This is the reason why Jesus, the apostles and their non-apostolic counterparts were referred to as teachers, and as prophets. Such a concrete understanding of the essential role of shepherds as witnessed in the New Testament means *poimenas* cannot be restricted to refer only to shepherd-teachers here as some scholars have assumed[16] because all the four references in this group gift, by virtue of fulfilling this role, were shepherds. The meaning of shepherd-teachers, or to be more precise, what shepherd-teachers did that distinguished them from other pastors must, then, be sought elsewhere.

---

15. Markus Barth, *Ephesians 4–6*, (Garden City: Double Day and Co. Inc., 1974), 438.
16. See for example Andrew T. Lincoln, *Ephesians*, WBC 42 (Dallas: Word Books, 1990), 250–251.

Barth seems to provide us with the place to look for its meaning, and that is the conjunction *kai* ("and") in shepherds and teachers, when its other meanings are taken into consideration. Although the most common meaning of *kai* is "and," the conjunction has a broad semantic range. As Greek lexicons highlight,[17] the conjunction could also mean "that is," "also," "namely," "both," "particularly," "even," "still," "and so," and "then." From *kai's* semantic range, Barth[18] pointed out that its most likely meaning in Ephesians 4:11 is "that is," or "in particular." Consequently, "shepherds-teachers" there could be rendered as "shepherds, that is, teachers," which accounts for our preferred dynamic translation of "teaching shepherds." If this is the case, then we should take it that it is actually pastors distinguished as teachers who were in view there.

We can then conclude that teaching shepherds were pastors who either gave the word of God mostly by way of teaching it, or, more probably, had a more pronounced ability to teach relative to other pastors. Noticing one's pronounced ability to teach the word of God relative to others may have been commonplace, as witnessed in the way people responded to Jesus according to the gospels. His teaching in the synagogue in Capernaum was noted relative to the scribes as one with authority (Matt 7:28–29; Mark 1:22). Since this authority must be directly related to his teaching, it most likely stood for his ability to teach as acknowledged by the crowd. Perhaps his teaching ability was manifested in the clear, insightful, and persuasive ways he taught which were unmatched by the ways the scribes taught.

The picture we then have of pastoral ministry from the New Testament is one of Jesus, as the pastor of Israel, exercising his pastoral ministry primarily through preaching and teaching God's word to the people of God. After Jesus's ascension, this primary aspect of pastoral ministry was sustained by the apostles, as pastors of Jews and Gentiles, and their non-apostolic counterparts who with them were variously designated as preachers and teachers, prophets, evangelists, and *presbuteroi-episkopoi*. The thread running through all these designations was preaching and teaching God's word. All the pastors, whatever way they may have been distinguished from one another, were teachers and preachers, fulfilling their pastoral responsibility of giving God's people his word. Filson was then right when years ago he concluded from his study of

---

17. See G. Abbott-Smith, *A Manual Greek Lexicon of the New Testament* (Edinburgh: T&T Clark, 2001), 15.

18. Barth, *Ephesians*, 438.

the New Testament that "every leader (pastor) of the primitive church was a teacher (and preacher)."[19]

5. The Purpose of Preaching and Teaching the Word of God
God's word, content of apostolic and non-apostolic preaching and teaching

So far, we have said nothing of the content of the preaching and teaching of apostles and non-apostles but simply assumed that they preached and taught the word of God just as Jesus did. It is important to establish that indeed they preached and taught God's word before considering the purpose of their preaching and teaching. We mentioned that Jesus's proclamation was the "good news" (*euaggelion*) whose content, we simplified, as the fulfilment in him of God's promises that he would restore the dethroned Davidic kingship by the *māšiah*. We pointed out that since Jesus as the *māšiah* was the promised Davidic king, not only was the Davidic kingship enthroned through him, but invariably God's kingdom too had arrived. This was why the good news was "the good news of the kingdom."

For this reason, after his ascension, Jesus became the centrepiece of the preaching and teaching of both the apostles and their non-apostolic counterparts. The good news they proclaimed (Mark 1:8; Acts 8:25)[20] was thus summarized as the good news of "Jesus" (Acts 19:13), or of "the Lord Jesus" (Acts 11:20; Rom 10:14–17),[21] or of "the Lord Jesus Christ" (Acts 28:31), or of "Jesus as Christ" (Acts 5:42; 17:3), or of "Jesus Christ" or "Christ" (Mark 1:1; Acts 8:5; 2 Cor 2:12),[22] or of "Jesus as the Son of God" (Acts 9:20; Gal 1:16; 2 Cor 1:19). At times a significant element of what God had achieved in, and through, Jesus, or a significant event in Jesus's life was given as the summary of the good news as follows: his sacrificial death on the cross (1 Cor 1:23; Gal 5:11; 1 Tim 2:6–7), his resurrection (1 Cor 15:3–4; Acts 17:18),[23] his unsearchable riches (Eph 3:6–8; 6:15), forgiveness of sins (Acts 13:38), the way of salvation (Acts 16:17; see also Eph 1:13), and peace (Eph 2:17). Nonetheless the kingdom of God as a summary of the good news was not entirely abandoned (Acts 8:12; 20:25; 28:23, 31).

---

19. Floyd V. Filson, "The Christian Teacher in the First Century," *JBL* 60, no. 3 (1941): 317–328, 322 – mine in brackets.

20. See also Acts 14:7; Rom 1:15; 15:20; 1 Cor 1:17; 15:1; Gal 1:11; 4:13.

21. See also 2 Cor 4:5; 2 Thess 1:8.

22. See also Rom 10:14–17; 2 Cor 2:9–13; 5:12–15; 10:14; Phil 1:15–18, 27; 1 Thess 3:2; Col 1:28; 1 Tim 3:16.

23. See also Rom 10:8–9; 1 Cor 15:11–12; 2 Tim 2:8.

Conversely, what the apostles and their non-apostolic counterparts taught besides the Scriptures revolved around Jesus, his preaching and teaching, and what God had done through and in him. The focus of their preaching and teaching was on his achievements and benefits, his words and deeds, his character and identity, and his locus and destiny. This phenomenon is well demonstrated in the content of the book of Acts and in the Epistles. We have glimpses of this phenomenon as well in a summary of what they taught. The teaching of Paul and Barnabas is summarized as the teaching of Jesus, that is, his words: "Then the proconsul believed, when he saw what had occurred, for he was astonished at the teaching of the Lord" (Acts 13:12 RSV). Since Jesus's supreme role was bringing the kingdom of God and which, therefore, as we highlighted, he taught about, it was also used to summarize what they taught: "He entered the synagogue and for three months spoke out boldly, and argued persuasively about the kingdom of God" (Acts 19:8).

However, because ultimately what the apostles and their non-apostolic counterparts preached and taught were all the messages of God through Christ and what he had done through him, their preaching and teaching contents were also summarized, in line with our earlier discussion of the same, as the word of God. Our conclusion is confirmed in at least four instances where the good news and the word of God are used synonymously. In the first instance, the preaching starting from Jerusalem was referred to as preaching the word (Acts 8:4; 13:5; 15:35; 17:13), which was heard (Acts 4:4; 10:44; 19:10). Thus its spread as they moved about preaching it and people believing it and repenting was described in terms of the growth of the word of God; "the word of God grew" (Acts 6:7; 12:24; 19:20). In the second instance Paul referred to Christ, the summary of the good news, and the word of God as the same (2 Cor 2:12–17). In the third, the word of God which Paul has been commissioned to make known was Christ, the summary of the good news (Col 1:25–28). In the fourth instance, the good news because of which Paul was imprisoned was referred to as the word of God (2 Tim 2:9). And in one instance, the word of God is pointed out to be the good news preached: "You have been born anew ... through the living and abiding word of God ... That word is the good news which was preached to you" (1 Pet 1:23, 25 RSV).

In the final analysis then, the apostolic and their non-apostolic counterparts, just as Jesus did, preached and taught the word of God as their primary pastoral ministry. But to what end did they do so? The answer to this question is crucial for it will throw into sharp relief the importance of preaching and teaching the word and thereby the reasons they should be taken as the primary activities of pastoral ministry.

Preaching and teaching the word for faith

It is clear that the purpose of preaching was to engender faith in Christ and what God has done through him. Jesus put belief at the heart of a proper response to the good news he preached: "the kingdom of God has come near; repent, and believe in the good news" (Mark 1:15). As I have shown in a previous study, this was because Jesus taught that it was through faith and repentance that one entered God's kingdom.[24] As we pointed out earlier, the Synoptic Gospels illustrate, as taught in the parable of the sower, that God's kingdom spread only amongst those who believed (Matt 13:18–23; Mark 4:13–20; Luke 8:11–15) and was hindered by unbelief (Matt 13:58; Mark 6:5–6). In John's gospel, Jesus taught that the way to eternal life, which as has been rightly suggested is substitute language for God's kingdom,[25] was to believe in him and his message (John 6:40; 8:24; 11:26; 20:30). Thus, where God's kingdom is mentioned in John, entry into it was to those born anew (John 3:3); an experience that was given only to those who believed (John 3:14–18).

Consequently, we can say that the purpose of Jesus preaching the good news was in order that people would believe it and, by that very fact, also believe in him. In so doing, the believers would be recipients of the fruits of his mission as subjects of the kingdom he brought that they had entered, and thereby begin receiving its benefits. These benefits are encapsulated in the summaries of the good news as revealed in the word of God – forgiveness of sins, salvation, peace, life, sonship/adoption into God's family, inheritance, the Spirit etc.

This purpose behind Jesus's preaching of the good news was maintained in apostolic and non-apostolic preaching. This is clearest in Paul's teaching to the believers in Rome. Desiring the salvation of his own people, Paul highlighted the place of belief:

> If you confess with your lips that Jesus is Lord and believe in your heart that God raised him from the dead, you will be saved. For one believes with his heart and so is justified, and one confesses with his lips and so is saved. The Scripture says, "No one who believes in him will be put to shame." For there is no distinction between Jew and Greek; the same Lord is Lord of all and is generous to all who call on him. (Rom 10:9–11)

---

24. Nyende, *The Restoration of God's Dwelling and Kingdom*, 179–181.
25. See Andreas J. Köstenberger, *A Theology of John's Gospel and Letters: The Word of Christ, the Son of God* (Grand Rapids: Zondervan, 2015), 285–286.

But rhetorically, in order to underpin the purpose of preaching the good news, he asked; "But how are they to call on one in whom they have not believed? And how are they to believe in one whom they have never heard? And how will they hear without someone to proclaim him?" (Rom 10:14). Preaching of the good news was, therefore, absolutely essential for bringing about faith in the Lord Jesus and what God had done through him. For that reason, those who proclaimed the good news were said to have beautiful feet (Rom 10:15).

In Acts, the purpose of preaching is concretely displayed. Because of this premium placed on belief and repentance, the narrator carefully informed the readers of numerous times people believed when the good news was preached: "But many of those who heard the word believed; and they numbered about five thousand (Acts 4:4; see also 5:14). Belief was also the outcome of Philip's preaching (8:12). This was also the case with Paul's preaching to the Gentiles (11:21; 13:12, 48; 14:1; 17:12, 32; 18:2, 8). Accordingly, we also have references in the Epistles of Paul where he reminded his audience of their belief on account of having preached to them the good news (1 Cor 3:5; 15:1–2; 2 Thess 1:10). In some instances, the narrator of Acts reports that when those convinced by the preaching of the good news asked for the appropriate response, they were told to believe:

> Now when they heard this, they were cut to the heart and said to Peter and to the other apostles, "Brothers, what should we do?" Peter said to them, "Repent[26] and be baptised every one of you in the name of Jesus Christ." (Acts 2:37–38)

> "Sir, what must we do to be saved?" They answered, "Believe on the Lord Jesus." (Acts 16:30; see also Acts 2:37–38)

However, we should not presuppose that preaching the good news to those who had already believed served no purpose. Preaching the good news – much like observing the Lord's Supper – would have helped believers to maintain, or recall, their faith in God for his unmerited favour towards them in Christ, making them continually thankful. The fact that there were problems of drifting away from the faith (Gal 3:1–2; Heb 6:6), and exhortations to persist in the faith (1 Cor 15:2; Heb 6:9–11; 10:23; 10:35; 12:3) support this view:

---

26. Repentance here stands too for belief because the two are inseparable. Belief precedes repentance, and there is no repentance without belief. We can easily relate these verses to Mark 16:16, if we take it to be primitive, that Jesus had promised the apostles that those who believed at their preaching and are baptized would be saved.

Preaching and teaching the word for growth

The purpose of teaching the word of God was for the growth of believers in knowledge and morality towards Christ – for discipleship. Growing towards Christ to eventually become like him was laid down by Jesus as the ultimate goal of those who followed him closely. They were to learn from his teachings and conduct and that is why each of the twelve was Jesus's pupil, which is what a disciple (*mathētēs*) literally meant. For this reason, Jesus said to his disciples that, "A disciple is not above the teacher, but everyone who is fully qualified will be like the teacher" (Luke 6:40). Since then good disciples were to be like Jesus, their teacher/master, he warned the twelve to expect the same treatment he was given:

> A disciple is not above the teacher, nor a slave above the master; it is enough for the disciple to be like the teacher, and the slave like the master. If they have called the master of the house Beelzebul, how much more will they malign those of his household! (Matt 10:24)

As a point in fact, in the Gospel according to Matthew, the apostles' commission to teach was tied to this goal of making disciples: "Go therefore and make disciples of all nations . . . teaching them to obey everything that I have commanded you" (Matt 28:19–20). A look at other relevant texts of the New Testament show that this remained the purpose for which the apostles and their non-apostolic pastors taught the word of God as captured in a mission statement by the apostle Paul: "It is he whom we proclaim, warning everyone and teaching everyone in all wisdom, so that we may present everyone mature in Christ" (Col 1:28).

In Ephesians, we have the revelation that Christ made apostles, prophets, evangelists, and teachers to be givers of God's word, or, in the words of Carson, to be involved with word-ministries[27] (see Eph 4:11). The ultimate purpose given in the Epistle for the giving of the word of God was the building up of the body of Christ by virtue of helping believers to grow and become like Christ, "until all of us come to the unity of the faith and the knowledge of the Son of God, to maturity, to the measure of the full stature of Christ" (Eph 4:13).

In this specific revelation, the growth towards being like Christ – the full stature of Christ – was in the realm of knowledge: knowledge of the faith, and knowledge of the Son of God. The definite article before faith (*tēs pisteōs*), as noted by Liefeld, meant the knowledge of "faith as a body of doctrine

---

27. Carson, "Do the Work of an Evangelist," 3.

(teaching),"[28] and not faith as belief/trust, which came from the word of God. Those without sufficient knowledge of the faith (and/or holding to false teaching) and of the Son of God were thus viewed to be in the childhood stage of their discipleship and thus subject to being swayed by deceitful and false teachings about the Son of God: "tossed back and forth by the waves, and blown here and there by every wind of teaching and by the cunning and craftiness of men in their deceitful cunning" (Eph 4:14 NIV). Teaching the word was therefore meant to help believers grow towards the same knowledge as Christ's in the understanding of their faith.

The same is alluded to in the book of Hebrews where the writer was frustrated with his audience for their lack of growth to the full stature of Christ in knowledge of the will of God: "For though by this time you ought to be teachers, you need someone to teach you again the basic elements of the oracles of God. You need milk and not solid food" (Heb 5:12). In contrast, those who were mature, to whom solid food was due, knew what was good (*kalou*) and what was evil (*kakou*; Heb 5:14). Since knowledge or discernment of good and evil was drawn from God's word (see Rom 2:18), it was only by being taught the word that his audience would grow and know God's will. Thus, the Hebrews writer had to press on in teaching them about the basics (Heb 6:1–3).

Although not explicitly stated, since morals and conduct are associated with belief and knowledge, the teaching of the apostles and their non-apostolic counterparts would have been designed to bring about in believers moral growth as well, towards the morals of Christ. This purpose should be obvious because there are aspects of God's commandments that directly speak on right conduct, attitude, thoughts and feelings that ought to be known and obeyed. Paul pointed out that jealous, divisive, and quarrelsome believers – those whose morals were not a reflection of Christ's – were infants in him. Using the metaphor of food, Paul wrote that they needed food fit for children in order to grow up to the measure of Christ. Correspondingly, since food was used as a metaphor for the word of God in the same way as in the Old Testament but, unlike in the Old Testament, not likened to pasture (see Matt 4:4; Heb 5:12–14; 1 Pet 2:1), their moral growth to become like Christ would be enabled by feeding on the word of God through being taught that word:

> And so, brothers and sisters, I could not speak to you as spiritual people, but rather as people of the flesh, as infants in Christ. I fed

---

28. Walter L. Liefeld, *Ephesians*, IVPNT (Downers Grove: InterVarsity Press 1997), 109; in brackets mine.

you milk, not with solid food, for you were not ready for solid food. Even now you are still not ready, for you are still of the flesh. (1 Cor 3:1–3)

Because moral growth towards Christ's standard was a critical factor in teaching God's word, non-apostolic pastors were instructed in various ways to model the word they taught the flock under their care. The *Presbuteroi-episkopoi* were instructed to set an example to the flock (1 Pet 5:3). Timothy was admonished to watch the way that he lived for the sake of those he taught (1 Tim 4:16). James alluded to exemplary living requisite for teachers on account of which he advised that few aspire to be teachers lest they be harshly judged (Jas 3:1). Pastors modelling what they taught from the word applied to the apostles since, going by the words of Paul, they themselves set an example in conducting themselves after their own teaching of the word: "Be imitators of me as I am of Christ" (1 Cor 11:1).

It is clear in the New Testament that food was occasionally used as a metaphor for God's word. Its teaching was therefore, in ways akin to what food does for the body, meant to promote growth in the realm of knowledge and morals in believers towards Christ's. This should not surprise us for Christ was the goal for the transformation of believers (Rom 8:29), and their destiny (1 John 3:1–3). The teaching of God's word was a vital means by which this goal was achieved.

The predominance of teaching and preaching the word of God together with the above purposes, then, distinguish them as the primary activities of pastoral ministry. Consequently, it is imperative that pastors invest in their abilities to do both, and diligently fulfil them as an integral part of their pastoral ministry.

4

Care for Those in Difficulties: An Integral Part of Pastoral Ministry

1. Introduction
Prophets and giving comfort

In our last chapter, we established that according to the light shed by the Bible, preaching and teaching are the primary activities of pastoral ministry. In this chapter, we widen our biblical perspective of pastoral ministry by examining an integral part of pastoral ministry which Jesus, the apostles and their non-apostolic counterparts, offered. Now, just like the primary activities of pastoral ministry, its integral component is rooted in, and reflects, a pastoral responsibility of prophets in the Old Testament.

In our second chapter, we pointed out that providing comfort (*naḥam*) to those in need due to their regret, grief, sorrow, and such like emotions was couched in the pastoral language of binding broken hearts (*šabar lēb*). These bitter and agonizing emotions would have been caused by difficult or traumatic circumstances. We demonstrated that "binding the brokenhearted" was the pastoral language used in the Old Testament to denote "providing comfort" because in the pastoral metaphor it was likened to binding wounded sheep as part of the care a shepherd gave the sheep he tended to. In line with this metaphor, God's people would almost certainly undergo difficult times and thus would need comforting, just as some sheep would invariably get wounded and need binding. For this reason, the binding of the brokenhearted ("comfort" from here on) was an integral part of shepherding, which in YHWH's plan for the leaders of Israel, prophets were designated to offer.

As we pointed out in an earlier chapter, prophets carried out this shepherding responsibility through two distinct ways. The first was through giving the people a timely word from God which in various ways brought them comfort. The second was through miraculous deeds which altered peoples' heartbreaking circumstances and thereby comforting them. Accordingly, as part of their pastoral ministry, Jesus and the apostles comforted God's people through both of these ways, as will be demonstrated below as we examine both in turn.

2. Comfort Through God's Word by Jesus, the Apostles and Non-Apostolic Counterparts
Jesus comforted God's people through God's timely word

Concerning the pastoral ministry of giving God's word, we have already seen that Jesus went about giving God's timely word because he spoke the word of God. His giving of God's timely word is best illustrated in the word he gave that God's kingdom had dawned upon the people of Israel. Those who believed his word would have been comforted because it pointed to a decisive change of, even a salvation from, their difficult circumstances towards life, peace, and joy, which characterized God's kingdom. Moreover, they would also have been comforted by their entry into God's kingdom thereby experiencing abundant life, peace, and joy. Indeed, this outlook is intimated in one of the gospel narratives. Typified in Simeon, there were those amongst the Jews who were waiting precisely for their comforting as God's people:

> Now, there was a man in Jerusalem whose name was Simeon; this man was righteous and devout, looking forward to the consolation (*paraklēsin*) of Israel, and the Holy Spirit rested upon him. It had been revealed to him by the Holy Spirit that he would not see death before he had seen the Lord's Messiah. (Luke 2:25–26)

Apostolic and non-apostolic pastors comforted God's people through God's timely word

Just like Jesus, the apostles and some of their non-apostolic counterparts who were prophets also gave God's timely word and thus comforted God's people. The Greek word for giving comfort is *parakaleō* as translated in Matthew where Rachel refused to be comforted (*paraklēthēsan*) because of the death of her children (Matt 2:18), and in Luke, where Lazarus was comforted (*parakaleitai*) in Abraham's bosom (Luke 16:25). The context in both instances is appropriate to the meaning of the word: difficult circumstances bringing about bitter emotions from which Rachel refused to have relief, while Lazarus received full relief.

But *parakaleō* has other meanings besides comfort. The verb also means to call. For this meaning to apply, the sentence in which the verb appears must have as its object the person being called with the context providing the reasons for their calling. *Parakaleō* also means to encourage or urge; a situation that points to a person being encouraged, or to the need for encouragement must be present for this meaning to be assumed. *Parakaleō* also means to plead, often with desperation, a meaning that would apply where the context shows a plea is indeed being made. Context therefore must determine which of the four meanings of *parakaleō* prevails where the word appears in the New Testament.

Accordingly, we have contexts of bitter emotions which support understanding of *parakaleō* as comfort granted through God's timely word given by apostles or their non-apostolic counterparts. For example, since the Gentile believers were troubled by erroneous teaching from some unnamed quarters, it seems as a consequence that they rejoiced on account of "the comfort," *paraklēsei* (as translated by the KJV), rather than on account of "the encouragement" (as rendered in virtually all other translations), that the message in the letter from the apostles and elders gave them:

> . . . and when they gathered the multitude together, they delivered the Epistle: (Which) when they had read, they rejoiced for the consolation. (Acts 15:31–32 KJV)

The letter, we may say, had God's timely word from apostles and elders by which they were relieved of their agonizing emotions brought about by erroneous teaching from a certain group of believers. In fact, the narrator points out that they were further comforted by Judas and Silas precisely because they were, like the apostles and elders, prophets: "who were themselves prophets" (Acts 15:32). As such they gave them God's timely word to the Gentile believers in many words (Acts 15:32): "Judas and Silas, who were themselves prophets, said much *to comfort* (*parekalesan*) and strengthen the believers" (Acts 15:33; my translation in italics). It should therefore be of no surprise that because prophets gave God's timely word, they were expected to comfort people as the apostle Paul clarified: "those who prophesy speak to other people for their . . . consolation" (1 Cor 14:3; see also 1 Cor 14:31).

Another instance that points to the meaning of *parakaleō* as comfort was when there was an uproar against Paul which affected those associated with him. His associates must have been anxious and fearful at the rise of the crowds against Paul in Ephesus which could have led to his imprisonment or even death. Their fears would not have immediately vanished after the tumult stopped. Paul therefore comforted them with what was likely God's timely word, rather than exhorted or called them as is often translated: "After the uproar had ceased, Paul sent for the disciples, and after *comforting* (*proskalesamenos*) them, and saying farewell, he left for Macedonia" (Acts 20:1; my translation in italics).

3. Jesus's Comfort of God's People Through Miracles

We turn our focus now to Jesus's pastoral ministry and subsequently to the apostles who continued to offer this ministry after Jesus's physical departure from the world. We shall consider the New Testament's meaning of miraculous deeds, albeit against the Old Testament's pastoral background we have alluded to, and discuss the way they were therefore an integral part of Jesus's and apostolic pastoral ministry. Finally we shall demonstrate that the essence of the pastoral ministry of offering comfort is care, so that giving comfort is essentially a pastoral ministry of care for those in difficulties.

Miraculous deeds of Jesus

In our last chapter, we pointed out that Jesus's work was characterized by preaching and teaching the word (Matt 4:23; 9:35; Mark 1:38–39; Luke 7:21–22; 13:32). What we did not mention is that apace with his pastoral ministry of giving the word were his deeds of miracles – healing and making people whole, exorcisms, cleansing lepers, raising the dead, and exercising power over nature. Indeed, in the Gospels, Jesus's main activities are summarily described not only as preaching and teaching the word, but also as performing miraculous deeds:

> Then Jesus went about all the cities and villages, teaching in their synagogues, and proclaiming the good news of the kingdom, and curing every disease and every infirmity. (Matt 9:35)

Jesus himself let his disciples know that alongside preaching and teaching, his miraculous deeds were an integral part of his work:

> He answered, "Let us go on to neighbouring towns, so that I may proclaim the message there also; for that is what I came out to do." And he went throughout Galilee, proclaiming the message in their synagogues and casting out demons. (Mark 1:38–39; see also Matt 11:2–5; Luke 13:31–32)

Care for Those in Difficulties: An Integral Part of Pastoral Ministry 75

Thus, alongside his preaching and teaching, his miraculous deeds constituted a substantial part of his pastoral ministry. In consequence, we have in the Gospels references to Jesus performing miraculous deeds (Matt 8:16; 14:35–36; 15:30; 19:1–2; 21:14; Mark 1:32–34; 3:7–11; Luke 6:17–19) as well as specific stories of these deeds as the following series of examples demonstrate.

With respect to healing, Jesus for example healed Peter's mother-in-law (Matt 8:14–17; Mark 1:29–31; Luke 4:38–39); he healed the woman with a bleeding problem (Matt 9:20–22; Mark 5:25–34; Luke 8:43–48); he healed the centurion's servant (Matt 8:5–13; Luke 7:1–10); and he healed the son of the nobleman at Cana (John 4:46–54). With respect to making people whole, Jesus restored the sight of the blind; of Bartimaeus (Matt 20:29–34; Mark 10:46–52; Luke 18:35–43), of a blind man at Bethsaida (Mark 8:22–26) and of a certain man born blind (John 9:1–41). He also made whole the invalid (John 5:1–18), the woman crippled for eighteen years (Luke 13:10–17), and the paralytic (Matt 9:1–8; Mark 2:1–12; Luke 5:17–26) so that they were all able to stand and walk.

With respect to exorcism, Jesus, for example, cast out demons with extraordinary results from a man in Gadara (Matt 8:28–34; Mark 5:1–20; Luke 8:26–39), from a child in the area of Mt. Tabor (Matt 17:14–20; Mark 9:14–29; Luke 9:37–43), from a dumb and mute man in Galilee (Matt 12:22; Luke 11:14), and from a dumb man in Capernaum (Matt 9:32–34). On cleansing lepers, Jesus cleansed a leper near Gennesaret (Matt 8:1–4; Mark 1:40–45; Luke 5:12–15), and ten lepers at a certain village (Luke 17:11–19). Coming to raising the dead, he brought back to life Lazarus (John 11:1–45), Jairus' daughter (Matt 9:18–26; Mark 5:21–43; Luke 8:40–56), and the son of the widow of Nain (Luke 7:11–16).

Lastly, with respect to exercising power over nature, Jesus, for example, multiplied food to feed thousands out of very little food (Matt 14:15–21; 15:32–39; Mark 6:35–44; 8:1–9; Luke 9:12–17; John 6:5–15), calmed a storm (Matt 8:23–27; Mark 4:35–41; Luke 8:22–25), walked on the sea (Matt 14:22–33; Mark 6:45–52; John 6:16–21), and turned water into wine (John 2:1–11).

Prophetic dimension of Jesus's miracles

Making sense of Jesus's miracles can be a complex affair stemming from, amongst other reasons, the modern world's difficulties with the authenticity of the miracles and the cures now possible with medical knowledge and technology. Consequently, the meaning of Jesus's miracles in biblical scholarship has been mostly sought and understood at a literary level as parabolic, symbolic, or even mythological, all of which render belief that they happened unnecessary to their understanding.

In response, we must note that although the miraculous from God may be unheard of, it should not be discounted. Miracles are logical on the basis that God, as revealed in the Scriptures, is almighty and the creator of the world. As such, they are not outside the realm of possibility. Besides, although uncommon, there exist testimonies of miracles (some of them documented) in the history of the Christianity up to the present.[1] We will therefore in our study proceed in establishing the meaning of Jesus's miracles on the basis that they took place: that they are historical, as reported by the gospel narrators.

There are at least three perspectives present in the Gospels by which one can make sense of Jesus's miraculous deeds. Awareness of these perspectives is critical to a better understanding of the meaning of miracle stories because it allows one to assess miracle stories from multiple standpoints. When viewed in this way, the content of the miracle story is what determines which perspective best makes sense of it. For this reason we shall briefly look at all the three perspectives even though the interest of our study is with the one which enables us to link Jesus's miracles to prophetic pastoral responsibility and, as such, to understand them as an exercise of his pastoral ministry.

Advancing God's Kingdom

The first perspective on Jesus's miraculous deeds is that they advanced God's kingdom. It is evident in the Synoptic Gospels that Jesus's miraculous deeds were understood as Jesus's work to advance God's kingdom through an all-out assault of the kingdom of Satan which was associated with disease, disabilities, and unclean spirits or demons (simply demons from here on). As I have extensively shown in an earlier study of mine,[2] it is his miraculous deeds of casting out demons that we learn directly that Jesus was waging a victorious war against Satan and thus advancing the kingdom of God as the *māšiah*. Jesus pointed this out when he said: "But if it is by the Spirit of God I cast out demons, then the kingdom of God has come to you" (Matt 12:28). Since the Spirit of God was his power (hence "finger of God" in Luke 13:32 as seen in God's mighty works in Egypt through Moses [Exod 8:19]), Jesus had been empowered by God himself to defeat his enemies – Satan and demons, in order to advance his kingdom.

---

1. See Craig S. Keener, *Miracles Today: The Supernatural Work of God in the Modern World* (Grand Rapids: Baker Academics, 2021).
2. Nyende, *The Restoration of God's Dwelling and Kingdom*, 161–174.

This perspective is illustrated in the Gospel according to Luke where Satan is directly singled out as the cause of the misery of God's people. The woman with a curved spine was under satanic bondage but Jesus freed her by his miraculous deed: "And ought not this woman, a daughter of Abraham whom Satan had bound for eighteen long years, be set free from this bondage on the Sabbath day?" (Luke 13:16). In the same narrative, Jesus's miraculous deeds of healing are described as delivering of people from Satan's oppression thus advancing God's kingdom:

> You know the message he sent to the people of Israel, preaching peace by Jesus – he is Lord of all. That message spread throughout Judea, beginning in Galilee after the baptism that John announced: how God anointed Jesus of Nazareth with the Holy Spirit and with power; how he went about doing good and healing all who were oppressed by the devil, for God was with him. (Acts 10:38)

The perspective of miracles as an assault of the kingdom of Satan is also illustrated in the view of demons as the cause of people's diseases and infirmities. Thus, Jesus healed people through his exorcisms of demons which was necessary if he was to advance God's kingdom. And so the epileptic boy was healed immediately when Jesus cast a demon from him; "But Jesus rebuked the unclean spirit, healed the boy, and gave him back to his father" (Luke 9:42; see also Matt 17:18). The seven women, one of whom was Mary Magdalene, were healed by Jesus when he exorcized demons out of them (Luke 8:1–2). Those troubled by demons were healed via exorcism (Luke 6:18; 7:21). Demoniacs were classified among the sick who were brought to Jesus for healing: "Jesus had just then cured many people of diseases, plagues, and evil spirits" (Luke 7:21; see also Matt 4:24).

The perspective that Jesus's miraculous deeds advanced God's kingdom is also present in John's gospel in the healing of the official's son (John 4:46–54) and making whole of the invalid by the pool (John 5:1–9). This interpretation is supported by their understanding to be signs (*sēmeia*). Just as in everyday life, signs in the Bible point to something else. In the Exodus narrative, for example, the miracles God performed were signs to Pharaoh that Moses had been sent by God to get the Israelites out of Egypt (Exod 4:1–17). In John's gospel, Jesus's miracles were understood to be pointing to the identity of Jesus as the *māšiah*. Thus the miracles were meant to help the Jews believe in him in line with their expectations that the *māšiah* will perform miracles to prove his identity: "When the Christ appears, will he do more signs than this man?" (John 7:31 ESV). This is also the reason why some of them demanded a sign from Jesus, "Then what sign do you do, that we may see and believe you" (John 6:30 ESV; see also John 2:18; Mark 4:11; Matt 12:38).

Since faith in Jesus was the means by which people entered God's kingdom (referred to as "life" on account of which it is seen as a Johannine alternative reference to God's kingdom),[3] his miraculous deeds, as signs, aided people to enter it. In other words, by engendering faith in him, miracles enabled Jesus to advance God's kingdom amongst the Israelites as captured by the narrator in reporting Jesus's miracle of bringing Lazarus back to life: "because on account of him (Lazarus, the sign of raising him from the dead) many of the Jews were going away and believing in him (John 12:11 ESV; see also 4:53; 9:23). This purpose of miracles is most forthright in the final chapters of the Gospel of John. There, the narrator points out that the gospel had a focus on the signs so that those who read about them would come to believe in Jesus as the *māšiah*:

> Now Jesus did many other signs in the presence of his disciples which are not written in this book. But these are written that you may believe that Jesus is the Messiah. (John 20:30–31)

Illustrating Jesus's teachings

The second perspective on Jesus's miraculous deeds evident in the Gospels is that they were a means by which Jesus taught. Several examples from miracle stories are illustrative. Jesus enabled the paralysed man to walk in order to teach the scribes that he had the power to forgive sins:

> "But so that you may know that the Son of Man has authority to forgive sins" – he said to the paralytic – "I say to you, stand up, take your mat and go to your home." And he stood up, and immediately took the mat and went out before all of them. . . . (Mark 2:10–12)

Jesus healed the withered hand of a man in the synagogue to teach the Pharisees that it was lawful to do good on the Sabbath (Matt 12:9–14). In our last example, Jesus miraculously enabled Peter, James and John to net a huge catch of fish after their all-night fishing ended in vain to teach Peter that he would help him to draw people into God's kingdom: "Then Jesus said to Simon, 'Do not be afraid; from now on you will be catching people'" (Luke 5:10).

---

3. For some explanations see Köstenberger, *A Theology of John's Gospel and Letters*, 285–286.

Offering comfort to God's people

As already alluded to, our concern is with understanding Jesus's miracles as his fulfilment of the pastoral ministry of offering comfort to God's people as the prophetic shepherd of Israel. This is the third perspective which is present in the Gospels and confirmed quite directly in Luke's narrative. When Jesus brought back to life the son of the widow of Nain, the large crowd which witnessed the miracle recognized it as an act of a prophet when they glorified God and said, "A great prophet has risen amongst us!" (Luke 7:16). What is more, Jesus had at the onset of his pastoral ministry communicated that he was the prophet whom God promised to perform miraculous deeds of bringing sight to the blind and freeing the oppressed (Luke 4:18–21; also Isa 61:1–2); all of which would bring comfort.

The view of Jesus's miraculous deeds as the pastoral ministry of a prophet to give comfort is also seen in the apt description of Jesus as "a *prophet mighty in deed* and in word before God and all the people" (Luke 24:19, my emphasis; see also Matt 13:54; Mark 6:2). We therefore turn now to discuss the way Jesus's miraculous deeds were actually part of his pastoral ministry of giving comfort to God's people.

Jesus's miracles and giving comfort

We have already noted the inextricable relationship between painful emotions brought about by difficult circumstances and providing comfort. Thus, one way whereby comfort was given is by a change of circumstances by means of which relief from the bitter emotions was effected. This pattern, the sequence of difficult circumstances spawning bitter emotions from which relief is then granted by change of circumstances, is present in most miracle stories of Jesus. In some of these miracle stories, there is specific mention of a bitter emotion (or of bitter emotions) that death, sickness, or some other difficult circumstance visited on a person or people before s/he or they received Jesus's miracle. The person or people were then comforted by the change of their circumstances brought about by Jesus's miraculous deed as we see in the following examples.

The first example we consider comes from a certain girl Jesus brought back to life. On account of her death, fear and grief are mentioned as the bitter emotions that her family were experiencing (Mark 5:35–43). The girl's death had made her father Jairus, the leader of the synagogue, fearful (Mark 5:35). Jesus was aware of this agonizing emotion and, given the miracle he was about to perform, was the reason why he told him not to fear but believe (Mark 5:36). The girl's death had also brought her relatives untold grief as witnessed by their weeping and wailing (*klaiontas kai alalazontas*) when Jesus visited Jairus' house. Just as was the case with Jairus, Jesus admonished them, indirectly, not to grieve because of the miracle he was about to perform. He assured them that the girl was not dead but asleep: "When he entered, he said to them, 'why do you make a commotion and weep? The child is not dead but sleeping'" (Mark 5:39). Indeed, shortly after, Jesus miraculously brought the girl back to life (Mark 5:41–42).

The common Bible versions use "amazed" and "astonished" to translate the response of those who witnessed Jesus's miracles (Mark 5:42b). The NRSV has "overcome with amazement." Both the ESV and GNB have "completely amazed." The NIV has "completely astonished," while the NEB has "beside themselves with amazement." Because they do not translate the Greek words that capture the peoples' response literally, these translations do not bring out, as intended by the narrator, the relief which Jesus's miracle gave those affected by the girl's death from their agonizing emotions. If we follow literally the Greek words for their reactions, we learn that the people were "out of their minds" or "beside themselves" (*exestēsan*) with great joy (*ekstasei megalē*) – "And they were out of their minds with great joy" (Mark 5:42, my literal translation).

The change of circumstances from death to life relieved the girl's father of fear and her wailing relatives of their grief, replacing them with mind-blowing joy. Mark's focus in this miracle story was on these contrasting emotions before and after Jesus's miraculous deed.

The second example we consider is Jesus making whole of the paralyzed servant of the centurion in Capernaum (Matt 8:5–13). The Greek verb used by the narrator to render the state of the centurion's servant, *basanizō*, communicates that he was in a terrible state of physical pain and, thus, psychological anguish. Indeed, the centurion's request for a miracle from Jesus was based significantly on the effects the paralysis was having on him of pain and mental anguish: "Lord my servant is lying at home paralyzed, in terrible distress (*basanizomenos*)" (Matt 8:6). The centurion himself was not insulated from the paralysis of his servant and its effects on him; he must have been anxious and grieving on their account. It is also possible that he feared losing his servant, a fear that probably would have been exacerbated by the thought of the prospective loss of a personal aid. For these reasons, he sought help from Jesus. The inference thereby is that Jesus's miracle of healing relieved him and his master of their agonizing emotions which their difficult circumstance had caused them.

The final example we consider is Jesus's miracle of calming the sea (Matt 8:23–27). In this miracle story, Jesus was asleep in a boat with his disciples when a great storm arose. The storm's strength was such that they feared their boat would capsize and they would drown. There was nothing they could do except wake Jesus up in the hope of a miracle, which he performed by calming the winds and the sea. Their fear thereby dissipated as they marvelled at Jesus whom they had seen perform miracles but not of this kind where the wind and the sea obeyed him (Matt 8:27).

We should note that even where there is no mention made of any painful emotions experienced by people prior to receiving Jesus's miracle, we are right to presume that sickness, disability, death etc. agonized their victims. The begging (Mark 8:22; Luke 9:38; John 4:47), the crying (Matt 15:22; 20:30–31), and the praying (Luke 17:13) for Jesus's miracle as well as the efforts taken by those who brought the sick or disabled to Jesus (Mark 2:3–5) are all indicative of agonizing emotions their situations caused. In a sense, given our own human experiences, we are stating the obvious. Physical or mental health, disability, and death spawn agonizing emotions from which we get relief when they are removed or their effects mitigated. The conclusion of our examination of Jesus's miraculous deeds in the Gospels is therefore clear: Jesus, the prophetic shepherd of Israel, was fulfilling his pastoral ministry of comforting God's people.

This conclusion is in line with Jesus's own, albeit indirect, self-description as "comforter" in the fourteenth chapter of John's gospel. In a bid to comfort the disciples who were sorrowful because he would soon not be with them (John 14:1–3), Jesus promised that he would not leave them as orphans (*orphanous*; John 14:18). Now, not having living fathers responsible for their provision and protection, made orphans both vulnerable to suffering and bereft of comfort. Jesus therefore was promising his disciples that his physical departure would, metaphorically speaking, not consign them into orphanhood. He would ask God to send the Holy Spirit who would comfort them: "And I will pray to the Father, and he shall give you another Comforter, that he may abide with you forever (John 14:16 KJV). In referring to the Holy Spirit as "another comforter" (*allon paraklēton*), Jesus was identifying himself as the one who had all along been their comforter.

4. Comfort Through Miracles in the Early Church
Apostles' miraculous deeds

Just like Jesus, the apostles performed miraculous deeds by God's power. According to Matthew's and Luke's gospels, Jesus first shared with the disciples the ability to perform miracles while he was with them physically in the world. In different ways, the Synoptic Gospels narrate the way the Twelve were given authority and instructed to perform miraculous deeds. Matthew's account indicates that they were able to perform virtually all the miracles that Jesus himself performed – healing the sick, making people whole, exorcism, cleansing of lepers, and raising the dead:

> As you go, proclaim the good news, "The kingdom of heaven has come near." Cure the sick, raise the dead, cleanse lepers, cast out demons.... (Matt 10:7–8; see also Mark 6:7; Luke 9:1)

Although we have no miracle story of the Twelve in the Gospels, we learn from the narrator of the Gospel according to Mark that the Twelve performed miracles according to their empowerment: "They cast out many demons, and anointed with oil many who were sick and cured them" (Mark 6:13). We also have evidence from the Gospels that the Twelve performed miracles besides the ones they were sent out two-by-two to perform. The man who brought to the Twelve his demon-possessed child for healing must have done so because he was aware that they performed miracles (although they could not cure his child as he wished, and so he turned to Jesus):

> When they came to the crowd, a man came to him, knelt before him, and said "Lord, have mercy on my son, for he is an epileptic and he suffers terribly; he often falls into the fire and often into the water. *I brought your disciples, but they could not cure him.* (Matt 17:14–16, my emphasis; see also Mark 9:17–18; Luke 9:38–40)

The twelve apostles continued to perform miracles after the physical departure of Jesus, narrated in Acts and hinted at in the Epistles, as the following catalogue of examples show. With respect to healing, many who came to Peter from areas surrounding Jerusalem were healed of their diseases (Acts 5:16). Publius' father on the island of Malta was healed of dysentery in answer to Paul's prayers (Acts 28:8) as were others of various diseases on the same island (Acts 28:9). On exorcisms, it is reported that Peter exorcized unclean spirits from those afflicted by them (Acts 5:16). Paul exorcized a "divining spirit" from a certain girl (Acts 16:16–18). The sick to whom pieces of his clothes (*soudaria/simikinthia*) were taken to had evil spirits exorcized from them (Acts 19:11–12).

With respect to making people whole, Peter made the lame man (Acts 3:1–10), as well as the bedridden man in Lydda (Acts 9:32–34) walk. While in Lystra, Paul made the believing cripple walk (Acts 14:8–10). With respect to raising the dead, Paul in Joppa brought Tabitha back to life (Acts 9:36–41), as he did Eutychus in Troas at a prayer gathering in the third storey of a building where the young man had fallen from the window to his death (Acts 20:7–12).

In other places in Acts, signs (*sēmeia*) are used to refer to miracles by the apostles, just as we saw they were for Jesus's miracles in John's gospel (see also Acts 2:22), albeit in combination with wonders (*terata*):

> Awe came upon everyone because many *wonder and signs* were done by the apostles. (Acts 2:43, my emphasis)

> Now many *signs and wonders* were done among the people through the apostles. (Acts 5:12, my emphasis)

Furthermore, Paul would testify how God used him to win over the Gentiles through the power of miracles – "signs and wonders" (Rom 15:19). He also stated that signs and wonders were a mark of his apostleship (2 Cor 12:12), and that they accompanied his preaching and teaching (1 Cor 2:4; 2 Cor 6:7; 1 Thess 1:5). All these seem to demonstrate that, alongside preaching and teaching the word, miraculous deeds were a characteristic of apostolic pastoral ministry.

Non-apostolic miraculous deeds

In Acts and elsewhere in the New Testament, we learn that others besides the apostles also performed miracles. If we take the longer ending of Mark to be original, it is clear as Jesus's pronouncement indicates that those who would believe in the good news would perform miracles:

> And these signs will accompany those who believe: by using my name they will cast out demons . . . they will lay their hands on the sick, and they will recover. (Mark 16:17–18)

Jesus's words in John's gospel that those who believe in him would do greater works than him also indicates the same since in John, "a miracle is a 'sign' (σημειον – *sēmeion*) and sometimes a 'work' (ἐργον – *ergon*)":[4]

> Very truly, I tell you, the one who believes in me will also do the works that I do and, in fact, will do greater works that these, because I am going to the Father. (John 14:12)

Although Jesus's pronouncements pointed to a prospective reality of all believers besides the apostles performing miracles, it was not absolutely the case when we follow the narratives and Epistles of the New Testament. This view is directly supported in Paul's Epistle to the church in Corinth, where he revealed that God had appointed some, not all, believers to perform miracles

---

4. Dorothy A. Lee, "'Signs and works': The Miracles in the Gospels of Mark and John," *Colloq* 47, no. 1 (2015): 89–101, 90, transliteration mine.

(*dunameis*), and some to be able to heal through their gifts of healing (*charismata iamatōn*):

> And God appointed in the church first apostles, second prophets, third teachers; then deeds of power, then gifts of healing ... Are all apostles? Are all prophets? Are all teachers? Do all work miracles? Do all possess gifts of healing? (1 Cor 12:28–30)

From Acts and James we learn that prophets, teachers, and elders-bishops – the pastors in the New Testament that we earlier discussed – were amongst the miracle workers and healers God had appointed.

Acts also reports that Stephen, the deacon and preacher, performed miracles: he "did great wonders and signs among the people" (Acts 6:8). There is also mention of Stephen's counterpart Philip doing the same, with the narrator specifying that he exorcized and made the lame walk (Acts 8:6–8, 13). Lastly, the narrator of Acts mentions that God did miracles, "signs and wonders," through the prophet and teacher Barnabas when he was together with Paul (Acts 14:3).

In the Epistle of James, instructions are given that open a window to see through and catch a glimpse of what pastors in the early church did, namely, perform healing miracles. In his very specific instructions, James exhorted the sick to call the elders-bishops to pray for their healing. In a practice reminiscent of what the twelve disciples did when Jesus first sent them two-by-two to go heal the sick when they anointed them with oil (Mark 6:13), the elders-bishops would anoint the sick with oil and pray for their healing:

> Are any among you sick? They should call the elders of the church and have them pray over them, anointing them with oil in the name of the Lord. (Jas 5:14)

Apostolic and non-apostolic miraculous deeds and giving comfort

The pattern we mentioned when discussing Jesus's miracles whereby difficult circumstances bring about bitter emotions from which relief is granted by miracle is also highlighted in apostolic miracles. The miracle stories of the apostles bringing the dead back to life point to the bitter emotion of grief which death caused them but from which they were relieved of by the miracle. In Tabitha's case, the narrator reports that the widows wept (Acts 9:39). These comments suggest a close, caring, and business relationship which the widows had with her. For this reason, their sorrow at her death was coupled with considerable anxiety. In the absence of Tabitha, they had lost both a source of clothing and a business aid: "All the widows stood beside him, weeping and showing tunics that Dorcas had made while she was with them" (Acts 9:39). The miracle of "resurrection" then offered them double comfort: relief from sorrow as well as anxiety.

In the case of Eutychus, great comfort is mentioned as the outcome of the apostolic miracle of bringing him back to life: "Meanwhile they had taken the boy away alive and were not a little comforted (*paraklēthēsan ou metriōs*)" (Acts 20:12). This remark about the effects of restoring the life of Eutychus can only make sense against a background of grief and sorrow which the death of the young man had caused.

Bitter and agonizing emotions are also highlighted in the mention of the apostle Peter's exorcisms by the narrator of Acts: "A great number of people would also gather from the towns around Jerusalem, bringing the sick and those tormented (*ochloumenous*) by evil spirits, and they were all cured" (Acts 5:16; see also Luke 6:18). Besides "torment" (NRSV's translation), the Greek verb, *ochleō*, has an array of other possible meanings including harassed, disturbed, troubled, confused, causing a tumult, and afflicted. What its meanings communicate then is that those from whom the apostle Peter exorcized unclean spirits were under some profound form of mental anguish from which they were relieved of by Peter's exorcism.

Thus, we can conclude as we did in our examination of Jesus's miracles, that in performing supernatural acts, the apostles and their non-apostolic counterparts were fulfilling their pastoral ministry of comforting God's people. And because signs and wonders alongside preaching and teaching the word characterized apostolic and non-apostolic pastoral ministry as they did Jesus's, they were an integral aspect of their pastoral ministry.

5. Caring for Those in Difficulties: the Essence of Comforting
Giving comfort as care for those in difficulties

Generally speaking, comfort is motivated by concern, compassion, sympathy and so on, all of which are aspects of care. To give comfort is to care for the ones who are undergoing difficulties. The link between comfort and care is evident in the Old Testament in places where the motivation behind comfort is revealed. For, example, when YHWH said through a prophet that he had comforted the Israelites, he immediately restated it by saying that he would have compassion on them because of their suffering. Compassion, in what was

YHWH's poetic word, was thus paralleled synonymously with comfort to reveal that it was the motivation behind YHWH's comfort of his suffering people:

> For the LORD has comforted his people,
>   and will have compassion on his suffering ones.
>   (Isa 49:13)

In another instance, YHWH likened his promised comfort of Israel to the comfort a mother gives to her child. The value of this analogy lay in the image it evoked of tender loving care behind a mother's comfort of her child. Thus, the promise of YHWH to comfort the Israelites was similarly motivated:

> As a mother comforts her child,
>   so I will comfort you;
>   you shall be comforted in Jerusalem. (Isa 66:13)

Care was meant to be the motivation behind the Old Testament prophets' pastoral responsibility of offering comfort to God's people but which unfortunately was absent. The prophets did not give the people God's timely word but instead they gave their own messages rather than caring; they were selfish, serving their own interests (Mic 3:5–7; Zech 10:2). They could not offer comfort to God's people because they were not concerned about them (see Jer 8:11).

In the New Testament, care for those in difficulties was reported to be Jesus's motivation behind his miraculous deeds that comforted God's people as the examples we highlighted. Jesus was moved with pity before he cleansed the leper (Mark 1:40–44). (The word translated pity, *splagxvistheis*, is an onomatopoeic word – from *splagxna* meaning the inner parts – which portrays a gut wrenching compassion or one so strong that it affects the body, underlining in this instance that Jesus was deeply moved by the suffering he encountered and responded with accordingly.) He had compassion on the crowd before he miraculously multiplied the available food (Matt 15:32). What is more, Jesus's comparison of his healing on a Sabbath with a father's rescue of his son fallen into a well on a similar day, indicated that care was the common factor in the two actions (Luke 14:1–5). Since care for one's son in a difficult situation was acceptable on a Sabbath, so was Jesus's care for the man in difficulties because of his withered hand. Jesus healed that man because he cared about him.

Indeed, going back to our earlier discussion of Jesus's indirect self-description as the disciples' comforter, Jesus comforted the disciples because he cared for them. Jesus himself made clear that he loved them with the greatest love in human life (John 15:12–17). What is more, his promise to the disciples that they would not be left as orphans presupposed the loss of care, such as the care children have from their living fathers, as their main concern when Jesus physically left them. Thus, Jesus's promise that in his physical absence, the Holy Spirit would care for them just as he did, resulted in their comfort when they needed it.

Viewed from this perspective, Jesus's and the apostles' pastoral ministry of comfort through giving God's timely word and miraculous deeds, was essentially their pastoral ministry of care for those amongst God's people who were in difficulties. Thus, the pastoral ministry of offering comfort, following the types of miracles that Jesus and the apostles performed, was in the final analysis a pastoral ministry of care for people in difficulties: the sick, the disabled, the demon oppressed, the hungry, the fearful, the leprous, and the bereaved.

With the link between comfort and care established, we can now proceed to discuss provision for the needs of widows and the poor as another way through which the pastoral ministry of care for those in difficulties was given in the early church. Discussing this additional way will make complete our understanding of care for those in difficulties as an integral component of what constitutes pastoral ministry from a biblical perspective.

Pastoral ministry of care for widows in the early church

The New Testament shows that the pastoral ministry of caring for those in difficulties was also carried out through providing for the needs of the widows. As a class of women, they were perpetually in difficulties. Places where widows are mentioned in the Old Testament indicate that women whose husband had died were faced with economic deprivation, oppression, and exploitation. The fundamental reason for this was that widows were denied a central source of wealth in pastoral and agrarian society, namely, inheritance (Num 27:8–11). Moreover widows without a son or sons and who were past child-bearing age were cut off from households which were an important unit for livelihood, protection, and justice.[5]

Therefore, to mitigate a widow's harsh circumstances, there were commandments not to oppress them (Exod 22:21–24; Zech 7:10; Mal 3:5) but rather to plead for them (Isa 1:17) and help them (Job 31:16). There were also commandments giving them rights to feast on tithes (Deut 14:28–29; see also Deut 24:17–22). To discourage their economic hardship and oppression, those

---

5. For a brief enlightening discussion of widows in the Old Testament, see Carolyn S. Leeb, "The Widows in the Hebrew Bible: Homeless and Post-menopausal," *Proceedings* 21 (2001): 61–67.

who victimized or neglected widows were stigmatized as evil. A person was considered wicked if s/he mistreated widows (Job 24:21), did not care for them (Job 22:9), denied them opportunities to seek justice (Isa 1:23), and robbed or murdered them (Ps 94:6; Isa 10:2).

Economic hardship, exploitation, and a generally precarious existence were the prevailing circumstances that encumbered widows prevailed into the first-century world of Jesus and the apostles. In his study of widows in the Gospel according to Luke – Anna (Luke 2:36–38), the widow of Nain (7:11–17), the persistent widow (Luke 18:1–8), and the poor widow (Luke 21:1–4) – Spencer captures this aptly thus: "all Lucan widows fit the basic stereotype of destitute, dependent women vulnerable to exploitation by corrupt authorities . . . and thus to deprivation of essential economic, practical, social, and emotional support."[6] Jesus himself specifically identified the issue of the exploitation of widows by religious leaders (Mark 12:38–40; Luke 20:47).

The backdrop above throws into sharp relief the significance of specifically singling out widows in the New Testament as a critical recipient of apostolic and non-apostolic pastoral ministry of caring for those in difficulties. In Acts, non-Jewish widows were not receiving food: "Now in those days, when the disciples were increasing in number, the Hellenists complained against the Hebrews because their widows were being neglected in the daily distribution of food" (Acts 6:1). This may have happened because of their double marginalization as non-Jewish widows. As Pao explained, "these widows were doubly marginalized, as they are not only 'widows' but also widows of 'the Hellenists,' who are outside of the center of power."[7]

We should note here that according to Acts the apostles took pastoral responsibility to provide for, or give oversight for the provision of, the needs of those in difficulties in view of their pastoral ministry. As the pastors of God's people who had the pastoral ministry of caring for those in difficulties, believers appropriately brought them money and material goods so that they could distribute it to, or share it with, those in need:

> There was not a needy person amongst them, for as many as owned lands or houses sold them and brought the proceeds of what was sold. They laid it at the apostles' feet, and it was distributed to each as any had need. (Acts 4:34–35; see also Acts 2:44–45)

---

6. F. Scott Spencer, "Neglected Widows in Acts 6:1–7," *CBQ* 56, no. 4 (1994): 715–733, 728.

7. David W. Pao, "Waiters or Preachers: Acts 6:1–7 and the Lucan Table Fellowship Motif," *JBL* 130, no. 1 (2011): 127–144, 138.

On this occasion, the apostles gave this responsibility to others by instructing that men be elected to be responsible for the care of widows and others in need. That responsibility was referred to as serving on tables, specifically, "to wait on tables" (*diakonein trapezias* – Acts 6:2). By giving this pastoral responsibility to others, the apostles were actually enlisting more pastors to their ranks to help in pastoral ministry.

Taking care of widows by providing them with food was a specific instance of the pastoral ministry of caring for those in difficulties which pastors were expected to offer. It was for this reason that those who were picked "to wait on tables" were also appointed to be pastors just like the apostles. This outlook is clarified by the criteria that was used to choose them, their being laid hands on, and their subsequent pastoral ministry.

The criterion that those the believers chose were required to be "full of the Spirit and wisdom" (Acts 6:3) was similar to what the apostles were required to first have before they began their pastoral ministry. It was only after the apostles received the Spirit that they began the pastoral ministry of giving the word through preaching and teaching, and of performing miraculous deeds. We should also note that being full of the Spirit is also mentioned as a justification for Barnabas' pastoral ministry in Antioch (Acts 11:19–26). Since Stephen and Philip were already full of the Spirit, they began to preach and teach (Acts 7:1–60; 8:26–40), and perform miraculous deeds (Acts 8:5–8); that is, to exercise pastoral ministry as pastors, as soon as they were appointed "to wait on tables" by the laying of hands (Acts 6:6).

We have connected hands being laid on them with their appointment to be pastors because, apart from being associated with healing (Mark 16:18; Acts 9:17; 28:8) and the gift of the Holy Spirit (Acts 8:17–18; 19:16), the laying on of hands signified a pastoral commissioning in the New Testament. So, Barnabas and Paul who were pastors had hands laid upon them (Acts 13:3) for pastoral ministry in Cyprus and Perga (Acts 13:4–12), and Antioch in Pisidia (Acts 13:13–52) as the Spirit led them. In another instance, there are indications that Timothy was appointed a pastor by the laying on of hands at which point, the context suggests, he received the gift of preaching and teaching (1 Tim 4:14; 2 Tim 1:6).

The pastoral ministry of caring for those in difficulties through providing for the needs of widows is also evident in 1 Timothy 5. The fact that caring for widows was in focus in that Epistle underscored it as an ongoing integral part of the pastoral ministry of caring for those in difficulties offered by apostolic and non-apostolic pastors. 1 Timothy 5 implies that Paul was concerned with the misuse of Timothy's pastoral ministry of caring for those in difficulties but with respect to widows. He therefore gave Timothy instructions to help him streamline that pastoral ministry. Accordingly, he instructed Timothy to ensure one thing: that he was only caring for widows indeed (*ontōs chēras*):

> Honour widows who are really widows. (1 Tim 5:3)

> Let the church not be burdened, so that it can assist those who are real widows. (1 Tim 5:16)

Paul must have been concerned at the misuse of Timothy's pastoral ministry of caring for those in difficulties through providing for the needs of widows. His instructions to Timothy were therefore that assistance was given only to widows who were without children (1 Tim 5:4) and past child-bearing age (1 Tim 5:9). However, Paul insisted that they needed to be women of faith (1 Tim 5:5) and good deeds (1 Tim 5:10). The requirement for widows to have no children and to be past child bearing age in order to qualify for Timothy's oversight care makes sense for these would be the widows who were cut off from households and thus with no livelihood, protection, and justice.

Pastoral ministry of care for the poor in the early church

It goes without saying that from time immemorial the poor are persons in difficulties. With insufficient or no means of livelihood, hunger is often endured if it is not a constant threat, while starvation is always a possible prospect. Having clothes and adequate shelter is a constant struggle for the poor. It should therefore be of no surprise that in the New Testament we find that providing for the poor was a way through which the pastoral ministry of care for those in difficulties was offered by the apostles and their non-apostolic counterparts.

The first example is from the Epistle to the Galatians where the apostles advocated taking care of the poor. In the letter Paul narrated a sequence of events that ultimately ended with his trip to Jerusalem where he met with the apostles and other leaders (Gal 1:11–2:1). At the meeting they recognized that God had entrusted to him the preaching of the gospel to the Gentiles just as he had entrusted Peter with the same to the Jews (Gal 2:7). Consequently, the apostles James, Peter, and John gave him their support to go to the Gentiles (Gal 2:9). But, they insisted on one thing, which was that he and his companions, Barnabas, and Titus "remember the poor" (Gal 2:10). In other words, as pastors to the Gentiles to whom they were going to fulfil the pastoral ministry of giving God's word, the leading apostolic figures pointed out that they had additionally to fulfil the pastoral ministry of care for those in difficulties through providing for the poor. The fact that they singled it out highlighted their view that care for those in difficulties was an integral component of pastoral ministry.

The second New Testament example we look at that shows that provision for the poor was a way through which the pastoral ministry of caring for those in difficulties is drawn from texts that concern themselves with an actual instance of Paul's practice. From Paul's Epistles to the Corinthians (1 Cor 16:1-4; 2 Cor 8 and 9) and to the Romans (Rom 15:25-28, 31), we learn that over a period of time, Paul made substantial efforts to rally his churches in Macedonia, Achaia, and Galatia, and other churches in Rome in Italy to give money that he would take with him to Jerusalem to provide for the poor. In Paul's own words, the money was "for the poor among the saints at Jerusalem" (Rom 15:26).

Although the collection he would gather from those churches would have multiple incentives – such as a repayment of debt (Rom 15:27), an act of grace (2 Cor 8:6), a gift out of love (2 Cor 2:8), equity (2 Cor 8:14-15), and for Paul, a gift back to his people (Acts 24:17) – the fundamental intention was provision to the poor. This view is firmly established in his identification of the poor as the recipients of the collection (Rom 15:26), and the collection referred to literally as (part of) his "merciful deeds" (*eleēmosunas* – Acts 24:17) which intimated that his gathering it was motivated by his sympathy for the plight of the poor amongst his people.

This is supported by Paul's defence of his pastoral ministry in which care as an integral part of it featured. When defending his pastoral ministry as an apostle, Paul told his church in Corinth that he was weighed down with care (*merimna*) for all churches:

> And besides other things, I am under daily pressure because of my anxiety for all the churches. Who is weak, and I am not weak? Who is made to stumble and I am not indignant? (2 Cor 11:28-29)

This is to say that Paul's efforts to collect money from churches to help the poor in the churches of Jerusalem were first and foremost out of his care for the poor in those churches. This care explains his dedication to gather money from a wide geographical area spanning the provinces of Macedonia and Achaia in the west, across the Aegean Sea to Asia and Galatia in the east. It also explains his passionate pleas to the churches to give, and taking time to articulate for them in his letters, theological rationales as to why they should give.

The final example of the New Testament we look at that shows provision for the poor as a way through which the pastoral ministry of care for those in difficulties was offered comes from Paul's own care of the poor as an integral aspect of his pastoral ministry. In his farewell speech to the elders (*presbuteroi*) of churches in Ephesus in Acts 20, Paul pointed out that preaching and teaching was an essential aspect of his pastoral ministry in Asia (Acts 20:18–24). He also pointed out that his pastoral ministry included provision to the poor whom he referred to in this context as those who were weak (*tōn asthenountōn* – Acts 20:35) because they were the recipients of his giving. As a point in fact, he demonstrated the importance of this ministry by adopting an exemplary lifestyle of working to earn a living (despite being a pastor with the right to be supported – 1 Cor 9:3–10) for the Ephesian pastors to emulate and thereby fulfil the pastoral ministry of care for those in difficulty amongst God's people:

> I coveted no one's silver or gold or clothing. You know for yourselves that I worked with my own hands to support myself and my companions. In all this I have given you an example that by such work we must support the weak. . . . (Acts 20:33–35)

To sum up, from the pastoral practices of Jesus, the apostles and their non-apostolic counterparts, which were rooted in the shepherding responsibilities of prophets in the Old Testament, we have seen that caring for those in difficulties was an integral part of pastoral ministry. As noted, the heart of this aspect of pastoral ministry was love; the care and concern by the pastor about those in difficulty which motivates the shepherd to actions that offer relief, or help, to the ones in difficulty. We can see this care offered through spiritual, faith based means, in the giving of God's timely word, and through miraculous deeds, while this care was also offered at a concrete, practical level, through material provision for those in need. Following this biblical perspective, it is incumbent therefore on pastors by virtue of love to faithfully care for God's people through both means thereby fulfilling this part of pastoral ministry which is integral to it.

5

Facilitating Worship: The Priestly Task of Pastoral Ministry

1. Introduction

We have so far offered a biblical perspective of pastoral ministry by demonstrating, first, that according to the Bible the primary activities of pastoral ministry are preaching and teaching, and, second, that care for those in difficulties is an integral part of it. We will complete our biblical perspective of pastoral ministry by examining what the Bible shows are its priestly tasks. First, we shall discuss the pastoral responsibility of priests in the Old Testament that was tied to the temple. We shall isolate these priestly tasks of pastoral ministry from that discussion and proceed to examine the ways that Jesus, as a priest, fulfilled them. We shall then conclude by examining the way the apostles and their non-apostolic counterparts carried out one particular priestly task, namely, facilitating worship.

2. Priests, Mediation, and Facilitating Worship in the Old Testament
Sacrifices, approaching God, and the mediatorial role of priests

According to the Old Testament, priests were servants in God's house (see for example Exod 28:43; Lev 5:6–7; Joel 1:13; Ezek 44:16). As such, they were called "God's servants": "Come bless the LORD, all you servants of the LORD, who stand by night in the house of the LORD" (Ps 134:1; see also Ps 135:1–2; Jer 33:21; Joel 1:9, 13; 2:17). Their association with service in God's house accounts as well for why they were referred to as "temple servants" (Joel 1:13; see also Ezra 2:43, 58; Neh 3:26).

As servants in God's house, the explicit work of priests was to offer sacrifices to God and help God's people in the temple with their sacrifices, as prescribed by YHWH himself through Moses (Exod 29:10–18, 38–46; 30:1–10; Lev 1–7). Specifically, only priests could sprinkle the blood of the people's sacrifices and take them to the altar to burn them (Lev 1:5; 21:16–24). One of the roles and importance of sacrifices was in their effecting communication with God so that, in the words of Ross, "the devout would come into God's presence on the basis of shed blood (and smoke from the subsequent burnt offering)."[1] Indeed, as highlighted in Eberhart's discussion,[2] the root for the Hebrew verb for "offering," qŏrbăn, reveals the place of sacrifice in effecting communication with God. He points out that a sacrifice as portrayed in the Old Testament:

> describes a dynamic movement through sacred space toward the center of holiness, and thus an "approach" to God. This movement reaches its climax in the burning (of the offering) which marks the transformation of the material offered by the individual or community, and "transports" it to heaven in the smoke ascending from the altar.[3]

Eberhart's discussion is in line with the content of the Bible as seen in instances where biblical literature is explicit that the smoke or incense (from the burning of a sacrifice) are communication to God. For example, in Psalm 141, a psalmist cries to God and equates prayer to incense:

> Let my prayer be counted as incense before you
> and the lifting up of my hands as an evening sacrifice.
> (Ps 141:2)

This is also the case in Psalm 5 although its sacrifice that is paralleled with prayer and not incense:

> O LORD, in the morning you hear my voice;
> in the morning I prepare a sacrifice for you and watch.
> (Ps 5:3 ESV)

In the prophets, the concept of sacrifices as prayers features prominently in YHWH's promises concerning his house being a house of prayer:

---

1. Allen P. Ross, *Biblical Worship from the Garden to the New Creation: Recalling the Hope of Glory* (Grand Rapids: Kregel Academic and Professional, 2006), 171. In brackets are my words.

2. Christian A. Eberhart, "A Neglected Feature of Sacrifice in the Hebrew Bible: Remarks on the Burning Rite on the Altar," *HTR* 97, no. 4 (2004): 485–493.

3. Eberhart, "Sacrifice in the Hebrew Bible," 491.

> these I will bring to my holy mountain,
>   and make them joyful in my house of prayer;
> their *burnt offering and their sacrifices*
>   will be accepted on my altar;
> for my house will be called a house of prayer for all peoples.
>   (Isa 56:7, my emphasis)

We also have prayers to God equated to incense in one of the visions of John in the New Testament where incense is said to be the prayers of the persecuted people of God: "the four living creatures and the twenty-four elders fell before the Lamb, each holding a harp and golden bowls of incense, which are the prayers of the saints" (Rev 5:8).

A person communicated with God through sacrifices, which made them essential to those who went to the temple, and casts into sharp relief the significance of the priest in their approach to God. Accordingly, the offering presided over by priests which God prescribed to his people afforded them avenues to communicate with, or "approach" (more on the choice of this word later), him for mercy, praise and thanksgiving, devotion, help, or communion.

Sorrowful for moral, cultic or ceremonial sin and thus in need of God's forgiveness or acceptance, the Israelites had the "sin offering," *hăttāth* (Lev 4:1–5:13). The offering was for the consecration of priests and Levites, as well as the altar (Exod 29; Lev 8; Num 7; 8; cf. Ezek 43:18–27). It was given for the cleansing of lepers (Lev 14), for the cleansing of the person who had come into contact with a corpse (Lev 20:1–3; Num 6:9–12), for purification after childbirth (Lev 12), and from unnatural discharge (Lev 15). The same offering was given every month (Num 28:11–15) but given twice in the seventh month (Num 29:1–6). It was presented during the Feast of Booths (Num 29:12–38), and the Feast of Unleavened Bread (Num 28:16–25). A sin offering was also given by the high priest once a year, on the tenth day of the seventh month, on the "day of atonement" (*yom kippur* from here on), for the forgiveness of the sins of the whole nation (Lev 16:11–28).

There was the "burnt offering" or "whole offering" *ōlāh* (Lev 1:1–17; 6:8–13) which was to be offered daily in the morning and evening (Exod 29:38–42; Num 28:1–8) and, on the Sabbath, alongside the one prescribed for the Sabbath (Num 28:9–10). Through this offering, they could dedicate themselves daily to God through this sacrificial gift which was exclusively YHWH's (see Judg 11:31). For this reason, it was the only sacrifice that was wholly burnt; no one received any part of it. To quote again from Hess, "the worshippers, by placing their hands on the offering, represent(ed) themselves in the victim and thus dedicate(d) themselves entirely to God" (mine in brackets).[4]

Offerings seemed to have also been associated with general approaches to God which included daily praises, and cries for help and mercy depending on the circumstances of the person who offered the sacrifice (see Ps 51:15–17). It may be for this reason that the burnt offering accompanied the annual Feast of Booths (Lev 23:4–8, 33–43), of Unleavened Bread, and of Weeks together with the New Moon festival (Num 10:10) because they were all occasions of thanks and praise.

For reconciliation, usually on account of social or economic wrongs against each other, the people had the "guilt (or reparation) offering," *āšām* (Lev 5:15–6:7; 7:1–6). They offered their gratitude to God and expressed their dependence on him for their daily bread through the "grain (or meal) offering," *minĕbāh* (Lev 2:1–16). Grain offerings were offered daily and seemed to accompany the burnt offering (Exod 29:38–42; Num 28:1–8). They thanked God and sacrificed for their health and safety[5] through the "sacrifice of peace (or thanks) offerings," *zebah šilāmîm*. Significantly, this was the only sacrifice that was a shared meal between God, priests, and the one who offered plus his invited guests (Lev 3:1–17; 7:11–21). For this reason, this offering, like the burnt one, accompanied the annual Feasts of Harvest (Exod 23:9–22; Num 28:27–31), of Weeks, and of Booths together with the New Moon festival (Num 10:10).

God's people could also present a non-prescribed offering to God either out of thanks, praise, or devotion to God, or in fulfilment of a promise they had made to God. They could offer thanks, praise or devotion through a "free-will offering," *nᵊdābâ*, and fulfil a promise they had given to God through a "votive offering," *nêder* (Lev 23:37–38; Num 15:1–3; Ps 54:6). Given their function to thank and praise God, freewill offerings accompanied the Feast of Harvest (Deut 16:10) which was naturally a feast of joyous thanksgiving.

Alongside assisting people with these sacrifices, priests also approached God in the temple on their behalf as portrayed in the symbolism of the robes the high priest wore. Having twelve stones on the breast piece and the names of the tribes of Israel etched on the shoulder stones (Exod 28:15–29) meant that Aaron and his successors approached God daily in the temple on behalf of the people of Israel: "So Aaron shall bear the names of the sons of Israel in the

---

4. Richard S. Hess, *Israelite Religions: An Archaeological and Biblical Survey* (Grand Rapids: Baker Academics, 2007), 187.

5. See a special note on this sacrifice in Norman H. Snaith, "Sacrifices in the Old Testament," *VT* 7, no. 3 (1957): 312–313.

breastpiece of judgement on his heart when he goes into the holy place, for a continual remembrance before the LORD" (Exod 28:29; also Exod 28:12, 21).

Presiding over people's sacrifices to God and interceding for them therefore give perspective on the vital role of priests in God's house: through sacrifices and prayers they mediated between God and his people. This mediation was also encapsulated in the instructions that YHWH gave through Moses that they should bless the Israelites (Num 6:22–27; Deut 21:5; Lev 9:22). By uttering to the people who came to the temple the words of blessing that God instructed them to pronounce, they would transfer to them God's protection, as well as his favour, grace, and peace all of which constituted his blessing. They were therefore intermediaries of God's blessings. For these reasons, they were essential to God's people; for their entry into God's presence and communicating to him.

Non-sacrificial temple activities, approaching God, and the managerial role of priests

There is more to the role of priests in the temple besides offering sacrifices and interceding, as follows.

i) Priests kept watch over the temple (Ezek 40:45–46; Zech 3:7) which also likely meant they were in charge of admitting people into the temple or denying them entry.

ii) Priests cared for the altar and kept its fire going for the daily reception of sacrifices.

iii) They had the duty of censing and trimming the wicks of the lamps, for they kept the lamps in the temple burning (Exod 30:7–8; Lev 24:1–4) and week by week they replaced the old bread on the table with new loaves (Lev 24:5–9).

iv) Priests helped people administer their sacrifices, which entailed talking to people in groups and individually on what was relevant to their sacrifices (Lev 10:8–11) and perhaps on issues of temple purity, as well as declaring the acceptance of their offering after burning it on the altar.

v) They also taught and instructed God's people on the law when they came to the temple (Mal 2:7–9 – hence the temple's association with God's law [Isa 2:3; Mic 4:2; Luke 2:46]), declared YHWH's saving deeds during the spring (passover) and autumn (Feast of Booths) assemblies which were grounded respectively in the Exodus and entry into the land. Moreover, it was logical for them to offer people instructions on the sacrifices they brought or on their cultic obligations.

   vi) They pronounced blessings on the people when they came to the temple (Ps 118:26) or before they left it (Lev 9:22; Num 6:22–27; Deut 21:5).

We also have references from the Old Testament that point to the temple as a place where God's people who were not far off came to bow down (*šāḥâ*) before him (Pss 5:7; 95:6; 138:2). Bowing down before God together with "serve," *ābad* – when understood metaphorically[6] – connoted not only submission and loyalty to God but also supplication to him. They also sang to him (Pss 27:6; 95:2; 137:3; Amos 5:23; 8:3), and regularly offered non-sacrificial praises and thanks (Pss 22:25; 26:6–7; 35:18) and supplications (Pss 18:6; 28:2; 65:1; 109:30) to him. In the course of their singing and/or prayers, they fulfilled, in some cases, the vows they had made to God (Pss 50:14; 56:12; 61:8). They also went to the temple to offer their tithes.

Those who lived too far away to go frequently into the temple would come to offer sacrifices during their pilgrimage for the annual feasts. During these festivals they sang their way in huge numbers into the temple (Pss 42:4; 68:24–25) where they gathered. There is even evidence that some testified of what YHWH had done for them in these great assemblies (Pss 22:22; 35:18; 40:9), while some honoured their vows before them (Ps 22:25; see Lev 27:1–8; Num 30:1–16). All these activities, which we may call "temple activities," were managed by priests who thereby enabled God's people to approach him in the temple.

Priests: facilitators of worship

Temple activities together with slain sacrificial offerings are typically referred to in English as "worship." Being in charge of temple activities and mediating between God and the people within the temple means that priests were responsible for both interceding for God's people and facilitating the worship of God by his people, or simply, for facilitating worship. As shepherds of Israel this was the second shepherding responsibility they had, even though, unlike the first we looked at in Chapter 3 – feeding God's people his word – it was not couched metaphorically in pastoral language (and precisely the reason why

---

6. See Edward J. Bridge, "Loyalty, Dependency and Status with YHWH: The Use of '*bd* in the Psalms," *VT* 59 (2009): 360–378, 363.

therefore we did not discuss it in that chapter). Together, they were indivisible pastoral responsibilities of priests as captured precisely in the blessing of Moses with respect to Levi from whom priests descended:

> And of Levi he said . . .
> They teach Jacob your ordinances,
>   and Israel your law;
> they place incense before you,
>   and the whole burnt offering on your altar. (Deut 33:10)

Under the worship facilitation of priests, the temple was thus designed to be the place for God's people to hear and learn from his word, to praise and thank him, to seek and find his forgiveness, and unburden themselves before him. It was also a place where God's people would also step into the transcendental and spiritual dimensions with, therefore, the ever-present possibility of the in-breaking of his power and revelations amongst them, and the experience of his subliminal presence variously in, for example, visions, comfort, thirst for righteousness, wonder, release, joy, and peace. Indeed, we have witnesses to this phenomenon in the love for the temple and sentiments towards it by some psalmists:

> O LORD, I love the house in which you dwell,
>   and the place where your glory abides. (Ps 26:8)

> How lovely is your dwelling place,
>   O LORD of hosts!
> My soul longs, indeed it faints for the courts of the LORD,
>   my heart and my flesh sing for joy to the living God.
> Even the sparrow finds a home
>   and the swallow a nest for herself,
> where she may lay her young,
>   at your altars, O LORD of hosts,
>   my king and my God:
> Happy are those who live in your house,
>   ever singing your praise. (Ps 84:1–4; see also Ps 122:1–2)

We find witnesses to this phenomenon in the epiphanies of some psalmists:

> As a dear longs for flowing streams, so my soul longs for you
>   O God.
>   My soul thirsts for God, for the living God,
> When shall I come and behold the face of God? (Ps 42:1–2; see also Ps 36:7–9)

> O God, you are my God, I seek you,
> > my soul thirsts for you;
> my flesh faints for you,
> > as in a dry and weary land where there is no water:
> So I have looked upon you in the sanctuary,
> > beholding your power and glory. (Ps 63:1-2)
>
> One thing I have asked of the LORD,
> . . .
> and to behold the beauty of the LORD,
> > and to inquire from his temple (Ps 27:4; see also
> > Ps 73:15-20)

We also find witnesses to this phenomenon and eschatological-like hopes of other psalmists to live in the temple forever: "One thing I asked of the LORD, that will I seek after; to live in the house of the LORD all the days of my life" (Ps 27:4; see also Pss 23:6; 65:4). We should add the promise of YHWH to Israel is another witness to the phenomenon whereby people would flock to the temple to learn God's law (Isa 2:3; Mic 4:1-3).

Since, as we mentioned, pastoral responsibilities of prophets and priests in the Old Testament equate to the pastoral ministry of Jesus and the apostles in the New Testament, we turn now to the ways Jesus and subsequently the apostles and their non-apostolic counterparts undertook these priestly tasks of pastoral ministry.

3. Jesus's Priestly Tasks of Pastoral Ministry
Jesus's intercessions and facilitating worship

We discussed in Chapter 2 New Testament literature which revealed that Jesus was a priest. As such he undertook the priestly task of intercessions. The book of Hebrews is particularly forthright in revealing that Jesus was a priest in the same way as Aaron was, but of the Melchizedekian order; an order superior to the Aaronic one (Heb 5:5-6; see also Heb 7:15-17). As such the author pointed out that Jesus interceded in line with his priestly tasks during his earthly sojourn when he interceded for people before God: "In the days of his flesh, Jesus offered up prayers and supplications, with loud cries and tears . . . and he was heard because of his reverent submission" (Heb 5:7). Indeed, we have a detailed prayer of Jesus interceding in John 17, which was actually his prayer as a high priest on account of its order, consecration, and God's name (which details we discussed in Chapter 3).

We should note here that although as a priest Jesus undertook this priestly task of pastoral ministry when he was physically in this world, the New Testament reveals that he continues to perform the task to the present, albeit in the spiritual realm, in heaven (Heb 8:2; 9:11, 24). As an eternal priest Jesus is able ceaselessly and eternally to make intercession for "those who come to God through him" (Heb 7:23–25). For this reason, no accusation against those in Christ can stand: "Who is to condemn? It is Christ Jesus, who died, yes, who was raised, who is at the right hand of God who intercedes for us" (Rom 8:34). Also, for the same reason, believers falling short of God's standards should not despair because Jesus intercedes (*paraklētos*) for them before God: "My dear children, I write this to you so that you will not sin. But if anybody does sin, we have an advocate with the Father – Jesus Christ, the Righteous One" (1 John 2:1 NIV).

As a result of Jesus's intercession believers are free from God's condemnation and thus are able to approach God in praise and thanksgiving, and in petition and supplication. This is clearly brought out by the very author of Hebrews who therefore encouraged his audience, on account of Jesus's priestly task of intercession, to "approach" God's throne of grace with confidence. The Greek word *proserxesthai* which is translated in English in the RSV as "approach," on the basis of its usage in the LXX, denotes prayers. (This informs our use of the verb "approaching" God in this study in the place of the more direct "communicating" to God.) Such prayers were those offered by God's people in the temple where God's throne was perceived to reside in the *debir* ("inner room"):[7]

> Since, then, we have a great high priest who has passed through the heavens, Jesus, the Son of God . . . Let us therefore approach the throne of grace with boldness, so that we may receive mercy and find grace to help in time of need. (Heb 4:14–16)

Thus the encouragement of the audience of Hebrews to approach God's throne of grace with confidence was actually a call for confidence in praising and thanking God, as well as petitioning and supplicating him as a result of Jesus's priestly undertaking of intercession.

---

7. For more on this word and its temple context see J. M. Scholer, *Proleptic Priests: Priesthood in the Epistle to the Hebrews*, JSNTsup 49 (Sheffield: JSOT Press, 1991), 91–95.

Jesus's sin offering and facilitating worship

Priests also offered sacrifices on behalf of God's people, and on the *yom kippur* the high priest sacrificed a sin offering for all of God's people. In undertaking the priestly task of his pastoral ministry by offering sacrifices, Jesus also sacrificed. However Jesus, as revealed in the New Testament, offered a single solitary sacrifice which was his own body, as a sin offering on behalf of all humanity for their forgiveness of sins. The book of Hebrews gives us the most direct elaboration of this revelation.

In Hebrews, the author reveals to his audience that the sacrifices that were offered by priests and high priests in the temple apparently did not secure God's forgiveness. It seems that God rejected the sin offerings they made in the temple thereby impeding or limiting, if not blocking altogether, their access to God. As a matter of fact, the author reveals that "it is impossible for the blood of bulls and goats to take away sins" (Heb 10:4). Accordingly, it is this shortfall of the offering of bulls and goats that made the sacrifices a repetitive affair:

> It can never, by the same sacrifices that are continually offered year after year, make perfect those who approach. Otherwise, would they not have ceased being offered, since the worshipers, cleansed once for all, would no longer have any consciousness of sin? (Heb 10:1–2)

Therefore Jesus as priest and high priest offered himself, his own blood, as a single once-for-all-time sin offering for the sanctification of those who believe:

> And every priest stands day by day at his service, offering again and again the same sacrifices that can never take away sins. But when Christ had offered for all time a single sacrifice for sins, he "sat down at the right hand of God" . . . For by a single offering he has perfected for all time those who are sanctified . . . Where there is forgiveness of these, there is no longer any offering for sin. (Heb 10:11–18; see also Heb 7:27; 9:12; and 9:26)

The Hebrews writer further highlights Jesus's self-sacrifice as a sin offering by mentioning it within the context of the heavenly assembly of which his audience, in some mystical way, were a part. They had come to Jesus through his sacrifice which had enabled them to be a part of the heavenly assembly. Against a backdrop of blood personification, the writer of Hebrews stated that the blood of Jesus had a better word than that of Abel, for his death was a self-sacrificial sin offering for humanity's sins, resulting in the forgiveness for those who believed; and was the reason they were a part of the heavenly assembly.

In contrast, Abel's death on account of being murdered by his brother Cain resulted in God avenging him (Gen 4:10): "But you have come to Mt. Zion . . . and to the assembly of the first born who are enrolled in heaven . . . to Jesus, the mediator of a new covenant, and to the sprinkled blood that speaks a better word than the blood of Abel" (Heb 12:22–24).

In the Gospel according to John, it is also revealed that Jesus as priest offered himself as a sin offering. We first encounter this in the narrative from the words of John the baptizer. In announcing concerning Jesus that "Here is the lamb of God who takes away the sin of the world" (John 1:29), John was drawing attention to Jesus as a sin offering which we examine in the following two ways.

The first way John drew attention to Jesus as a sin offering by calling him the lamb of God is straight forward. Since lambs were sacrificed as sin offerings (Lev 4:32), Jesus as a lamb was going to be sacrificed for the sins of the world. This understanding is captured well in Paul's second letter to the Corinthians concerning Jesus, who as a sin offering-lamb was made sin for the sake of believers: "For our sake he made him to be sin who knew no sin, so that in him we might become the righteousness of God" (2 Cor 5:21; see also Eph 5:2). It is also alluded to in Colossians where temple terminology is used to refer to the effects of Jesus's body thus pointing to it as a sin offering: "he has now reconciled in his fleshly body through death, so as to present you holy and blameless and irreproachable before him . . ." (Col 1:22; see also Eph 1:7).

Jesus as a lamb sin offering is also revealed in the book of Revelation where he is so predominantly referred to as "the Lamb," *to arnion* (e.g. Rev 6:1; 14:1; 17:14) – twenty-nine times according to Aune's study[8] – to the extent that it is essentially his title in the apocalypse. The title as a symbol of Jesus's self-sacrificial sin offering is pointed out in the remarks about the Lamb's slaying. So, for example, when John saw the lamb standing, the mark of its slaying, sometime in the past, was still visible: ". . . a lamb standing as having been slain" (Rev 5:6; see also 5:9, 12; 13:8). As Aune clarifies,[9] the adjectival participle "like/as" having been slain, *hos hesphagmenon*, signified that the lamb did not just appear as if slain, but having been actually slaughtered, was now still alive. The verb itself, "having been slain" (*hesphagmenon*) being in the perfect tense communicated the slaying, a past action, had current consequences. For these reasons John's vision of the lamb as if it was slain signified both Jesus's self-sacrificial sin offering and his subsequent resurrection which together

---

8. David E. Aune, *Revelation 1–5*, WBC 52A (Nashville: Thomas Nelson, 1997), 352.
9. Aune, *Revelation 1–5*, 353.

pointed to the ongoing efficacy of his sin offering. This ongoing efficacy of Jesus's past sacrifice is seen in the lives of those who had passed through the tribulation for they had cleansed themselves with his blood at a time when Jesus was already in the heavens (where in fact they had met him): "These are they who have come out of the great ordeal; they have washed their robes and made them white in the blood of the lamb" (Rev 7:14).

The second way John drew attention to Jesus as a sin offering by calling him the lamb of God is based on the parallelism (but with some variations) between the outcomes of Jesus's death as lamb and those of the death of the passover lamb (Exod 12:26–27), which then make Jesus a paschal lamb – "our paschal lamb" (1 Cor 5:7) – for the first Christians. These parallels[10] are as follows:

Passover	Last Supper
1. Interpretation given for the meal (Exod 12:26–27).	Jesus gives interpretation of bread and wine.
2. Unleavened bread interpreted as "the bread of affliction" (Deut 16:3), and later "this is the poor bread that our ancestors ate in Egypt."[11]	Jesus interprets the bread as "this is my body" (Mark 14:22; Matt 26:26).
3. Cups of wine shared in celebration.[12]	Jesus interprets the cup of wine as "my blood of the covenant, which is poured out for many for the forgiveness of sins (Matt 26:28; Mark 14:24).
4. The meal is a memorial of God's deliverance from Egypt (Exod 12:24).	Jesus instructs the meal be eaten as a memorial of his sacrificial death (Luke 22:19; 1 Cor 11:24–26).

In an astonishing turn of events, then, the Passover meal was transformed into a meal that no longer looked back to the past but, fixed on the present, looked forward to an imminent event. It was to that imminent event that in future, following Jesus's instructions, the meal would be used to look back to and commemorate. In other words, it became a meal about Jesus and what his death would achieve which included forgiveness of sins. This turn of events meant that that Passover lamb was, unlike the typical ones, a sin offering. France articulates it thus:

---

10. For a brief discussion on the parallels, see Joel Marcus, "Passover and Last Supper Revisited," *NTS* 59, no. 4 (2013): 303–324.

11. From the Passover Haggadah quoted in Marcus, "Passover," 315.

12. Four cups of wine were to be served according to the Mishnah (*b. Pesaḥ 10:1–7*).

In the context of the Passover meal, the memorial of the rescue of God's covenant people from slavery and of the lamb whose death was a necessary part of their deliverance, these words [which Jesus spoke during the meal] gave the disciples a whole new dimension against which to set Jesus's insistent prediction that he had come to Jerusalem to die.[13]

The outcome of Jesus's sacrificial death was the enabling of those who believe to approach God. This is clear, again, in Hebrews where the writer spoke of the confidence with which he and fellow believers had in entering God's sanctuary (his presence, we shall return to this later) because of Jesus's blood which had made God accessible:

> Therefore, my friends, since we have confidence to enter the sanctuary by the blood of Jesus, by the new and living way that he opened for us the curtain (that is, through his flesh). (Heb 10:19–20)

Reference to "accessing" God by opening of the curtain (which made the *debir*, where God's throne was inaccessible, except for the High Priest who went there once a year on the *yom kippur*) is also found in the Gospels where the narrators mention that the temple curtain was torn at the death of Jesus:

> Then Jesus gave a loud cry and breathed his last. And the curtain of the temple was torn into two, from top to bottom. (Mark 15:37–38; also Matt 27:51; Luke 23:45)

This phenomenon was precisely as a result of his sin offering which, as soon as he offered himself, made it possible for people to approach God directly without encumbrances. The same is alluded to in the Epistle to the Ephesians where the blood of Jesus is said to bring both believing Gentiles and Jews near to God (Eph 2:13).

Jesus's priesthood and facilitating worship through its delocalization

As we have seen already, Jesus's priestly tasks of his pastoral ministry made slain sacrifices as avenues of approaching God (the temple as the special locale for accessing God) redundant. Delocalizing of access to God due to Jesus's priestly pastoral ministry is clearest in the Gospel of John.

---

13. R. T. France, *The Gospel of Mark*, NIGTC (Grand Rapids: Eerdmans, 2002), 563.

In a recent study,[14] I argued that the conversation Jesus had with the Samaritan woman was, at heart, about the location at which to approach God. The Samaritan woman brought it up when she sensed that Jesus was a prophet (John 4:19) thus: "Our ancestors worshiped (*prosekunēsan*) on this mountain, but you say the place where people must worship (*proskunein*) is in Jerusalem" (John 4:20). I pointed out that the Greek word in the LXX, for worship, *proskunein*, literally means "to bow down." Since bowing down in Old Testament literature is done predominantly before a deity at a location where the deity is accessible (e.g. Exod 20:5; Lev 26:1; Num 22:31; Deut 4:19; Joshua 23:7; 1 Kgs 19:18), *proskunein* signified the accessing of God in the temple where he resided.[15] The woman then was unsure who between the Jews and Samaritans was right about the place to go to access God; whether it was Mt. Gerizim or the temple in Jerusalem.

In response, Jesus indirectly alerted the woman that access to God was through him, thus qualifying as the temple of God:

> But the hour is coming, and is now here, when true worshipers will worship the Father in spirit and truth, for the Father seeks such as these to worship him. God is spirit, and those who worship him must worship him in spirit and truth. (John 4:23–24)

Jesus revealed that the time had arrived when neither Mt. Gerizim nor the temple were the places to access God; God would be accessed in "Spirit and truth" (*pneumati kai alētheia*), both of which had to do with Jesus. The meaning of truth in the Gospel of John had its common sense (reality/genuineness), but also a moral sense (acting uprightly/righteous acts), and a revelatory sense (disclose/make known),[16] all of which were centred on Jesus (John 1:17; 14:6; 8:32; 8:45). Since those who believed in him were enabled by his priesthood to access God, accessing God "in truth" was in essence doing so in, or through, Jesus.

As for "spirit," the reference in John is generally to the Holy Spirit which, or who, is linked intimately with Jesus. He descended upon him (John 1:32) before he began to fulfil his destiny; he would take over after Jesus's physical departure as "another companion" (*allon paraklēton*, John 14:16), to guide the disciples into the truth (John 16:13), revealing to them Jesus's and the Father's truth (John 16:14–15). Jesus would also baptize believers with the Spirit (John

---

14. Peter Nyende, *The Restoration of God's Dwelling and Kingdom: A Biblical Theology* (Carlisle: Langham Global Library, 2023), 223–225.

15. See footnote 7 for a reference on this word.

16. See Dennis R. Lindsay, "What is Truth? Ἀλήθεια in the Gospel of John," *ResQ* 35, no. 3 (1993): 129–145.

1:33) which would also be given to them (John 7:39). In view of Jesus's priesthood and its accomplishments, this then reveals that approaching God "in spirit" was essentially doing so in, or through, Jesus.

The effects then of Jesus's priesthood were to delocalize the access of God from the temple, or any other place for that matter, to wherever men and women who believed in him were. To quote from my previous study:

> Through Jesus believers could access God anywhere for Jesus would be present everywhere by the Spirit who was promised to all those who believed in him. To put it differently, in Jesus, believers would have the Spirit by virtue of which they would approach God wherever they were. This interpretation is well portrayed in GNB's rendering of the Greek text thus: "God is Spirit, and only by the power of his Spirit can people worship him as he really is." (John 4:24 GNB)[17]

For this reason, it was through or in Jesus (or in his name) that believers anywhere would petition God in prayers:

> On that day you will ask nothing of me. Very truly I tell you if you ask anything of the Father, in my name, he will give to you. Until now you have not asked anything in my name. Ask and you will receive so that your joy may be full (John 16:23–24; see also John 15:7; 15:16; 16:23–24).

This outlook is also present in Ephesians where it is revealed that believers through Jesus have access to God by his Spirit: "for through him both of us have access in one Spirit to the Father" (Eph 2:18; see also Eph 3:12). The fact that the context of this statement, as Lincoln points out,[18] is sacrificial imagery first alluded to in verse 13, signifies the delocalization of access to God from the temple to wherever those who believe are because they approach God in Jesus. Delocalized access to God is also seen in the admonition to the audience of Hebrews in view of Jesus sacrificial death "outside the camp" (Heb 13:11–12). Through him therefore, they are exhorted to offer God praise and thanks through the "fruit of their lips" wherever they are: "Through him (Jesus), then, let us continually offer a sacrifice of praise to God which is the

---

17. Nyende, *Restoration of God's Dwelling and Kingdom*, 224–225.

18. Andrew T. Lincoln, *Ephesians*, Word Biblical Commentary 42 (Dallas: Word Publishers, 1990), 149.

fruit of our lips that confess his name"[19] (Heb 13:15; see also 1 Pet 2:5). In the past, they would have done so, but in ways limited to the temple and to actual material sacrifices, "through the fruits of their produce," i.e. a grain (or meal) offering *minĕbāh*, or the sacrifice of peace (or thanks), *zebah šilāmîm*, which accompanied the annual Feasts of Harvest.

4. The Priestly Task of Pastoral Ministry in the Early Church

Jesus's priesthood therefore rendered unnecessary the facilitation of approaching God through slain sacrifices in the temple, or any other place, as a priestly task of pastoral ministry. As a result, Jesus did not commission the apostles to continue after him with this priestly task – as he had done with his pastoral ministry of preaching and teaching, and of care for those in difficulties. Thus, the apostles and their non-apostolic counterparts did not undertake to offer slain sacrifices on behalf of God's people as a part of their priestly task. Rather, the priestly task of their pastoral ministry was limited to facilitating non-sacrificial worship as we detail below.

Temple activities reproduced in activities of Christian gatherings

There is evidence from the New Testament that after Jesus's ascension Christians regularly assembled together – they regularly "gathered," *ekklēsia* (although *sunagōgē* [Acts 15:30; Jas 2:2] and *sunathroizō* [Acts 12:12] are occasionally used too). In the narrative of Acts, for example, believers gathered around the apostles (Acts 2:42; 2:44; 5:12; 13:44) or gathered together under their charge (Acts 11:26; 15:30), or simply gathered by themselves (Acts 12:12; 14:27). In Paul's first letter to the church in Corinth he mentioned their gathering together as a typical affair (1 Cor 5:4; 11:17; 14:26). Assembling together is also implied as a typical affair with believers who were the recipients of James' letter (Jas 2:2). This state of affairs corresponds with the exhortation of the writer of Hebrews to his audience not to neglect the gatherings: "not neglecting to meet together, as is the habit of some, but encouraging one another, and all the more as you see the Day approaching" (Heb 10:25).

Gatherings of Christians were prevalent to the extent that *ekklēsia* came to be used to refer to a group of Christians in a particular place, e.g. "the church in Jerusalem" (Acts 8:1; 11:22; see also Rom 16:1; 1 Cor 1:2; 10:32), or,

---

19. On explaining the meaning of "confessing his name" as praise, see James Swetnam, "ὁ ἀπόστολος in Hebrews 3:1," *Bib* 89, no. 2 (2008): 255–259.

in the plural, to refer to groups of Christians in all, or various, places, e.g. "the churches of Macedonia" (2 Cor 8:1; see also Rom 16:4; Gal 1:2; 1 Thess 2:14; 2 Thess 1:4). Calling a group of believers an *ekklesia* underscored that gathering together characterized the life of the group; the term applied concretely to Christians in various places because they met together regularly.

The activities in Christian gatherings, apart from the eating of the Lord's Supper, were similar to the temple activities we earlier examined and classified as worship. Prayer was a first of the activities of Christian assemblies as we see in the following examples. In Acts when they gathered together around the disciples, they prayed (Acts 2:42). When they gathered in the house of Mary, they were praying (Acts 12:12). Paul's instructions to the church in Corinth that women should have their heads covered when they prayed (1 Cor 11:2–16) makes sense if prayers were usually offered in those gatherings. He also exhorted individuals in the church not to pray in tongues when they gathered together unless someone could interpret them (1 Cor 14:13–19). (Praying in tongues were unhelpful in leading the gathered people in prayer because they could not understand the prayers.) And in his pastoral letter to Timothy, Paul instructed him when the church he was responsible for gathered to have prayers offered for all people particularly those in power (1 Tim 2:1–2). He gave more guidance to Timothy on the subject of prayers in the assembly by instructing that, prior to praying and when praying, men in the assemble should not quarrel or be upset with each other: "in every place the men should pray, lifting up holy hands without anger or argument" (1 Tim 2:8).

A second activity in Christian gatherings was listening to, and being given lessons from, the word of God. Acts narrates that the early Christians gathered to hear the apostles' teaching (Acts 2:42) which, as we demonstrated in Chapter 3 was the word of God. The same book shows Paul preaching the whole night to the gathering in Troas (Acts 20:7–12). Paul himself testified that he never tired of teaching and preaching the word when they assembled in both public places as well as in their houses (Acts 20:20). In addition, Paul highlighted, in his letter to the church in Corinth, that the giving of God's word in the various forms alluded to was a predominant activity of Christian gatherings:

> When you come together, each one has a hymn, *a lesson, a revelation, a tongue, or an interpretation*. Let all things be done for building up. (1 Cor 14:26, my emphasis)

In the Pastorals, Paul specifically instructed Timothy to read, proclaim, and teach Scripture which, judging from what follows the passage in verse 16, was in the context of Christian assemblies. This is why the word "public" is supplied in some translations of this verse: "attend to the public reading of Scripture, to preaching, to teaching" (1 Tim 4:13 RSV). We also know from the New Testament that the letters of the apostles were read out loud in the gatherings as the word of God (Col 4:16; 1 Thess 5:27). The letter to the Hebrews stands out in this regard because it was described as "a word of exhortation" (*logos tēs paraklēseōs* – Heb 13:22) which meant that it was a sermon (see Acts 13:15) meant to be read out in the church assembly of his audience. The letter of James also adds to our literary evidence of reading of Scriptures in the assembly by intimating that the mode of exposure to Scriptures in the assemblies was primarily by hearing: "But be doers of the word, and not merely hearers who deceive themselves" (Jas 1:22).

A third activity in Christian gatherings was singing. It was mentioned by Paul in the list of activities in Christian gathering which he highlighted to the church in Corinth (1 Cor 14:26): "When you come together, each one has *a hymn*, a lesson, a revelation, a tongue, or an interpretation" (1 Cor 14:26). In Ephesians we learn that besides hymns, there were other types of singing in Christian gatherings. There were psalms (*psalmois*), and spiritual songs (*ōdais pneumatikais*): "but be filled with the Spirit as you sing psalms and hymns and spiritual songs amongst yourselves, singing and making melody to the Lord . . ." (Eph 5:18–19).

A fourth activity in Christian gatherings was giving. We have evidence of giving as an integral part of the activities in Christian gatherings very early in the life of the first Christians. In Acts, the narrator mentions specifically the giving of Christians in their initial gatherings (see Acts 4:34–35). We have more on giving in the early church in the letters of Paul. In his first letter to the Corinthians, Paul shares a plan of giving with the church in Corinth that entailed their giving every first day of the week when they met in advance of his visit during which he would receive their collection: "On the first day of the week, each of you is to put aside and save whatever extra you earn, so that collections need not to be taken when I come" (1 Cor 16:2). As we pointed out in our last chapter, Paul collected an offering from churches in order to take it to the poor believers in Jerusalem. Paul would again talk about the same collection in his second letter to the church in Corinth when he encouraged them to be cheerful givers for God loved such (2 Cor 9:6–7), and assured them of God's provision and blessings because of their giving (2 Cor 9:8–10).

Temple activities substituted with activities of Christians gatherings

As should be clear by now, activities in Christian assemblies mirrored temple activities. The resemblances were not incidental but a phenomenon that pointed to the transfer, and meaning thereof, of temple activities to activities of Christian gatherings. The use of temple terminology by the apostles and their non-apostolic counterparts to refer to the activities in Christian gatherings supports this view. By using temple terminology, the apostles intentionally applied the understandings of temple activities to activities in Christian gatherings and the designated roles of priests in the temple to understand their roles in those gatherings. So, for example, giving in Christian assemblies was looked upon as a sacrificial offering. In his letter to the Philippians, Paul referred to the giving of Christians as "a fragrant offering, a sacrifice acceptable and pleasing to God" (Phil 4:18). In Hebrews, the writer mentioned doing good (*eupoias*) and sharing (*kōinonias*) – both of which took place in Christian gatherings – as sacrifices that were pleasing to God: "Do not neglect to do good and to share what you have, for such sacrifices are pleasing to God" (Heb 13:16).

There are more examples of giving on Christian gatherings viewed as sacrificial offerings. By describing gifts as freely offered, the apostles were substituting them for the "free-will offering," *nᵊḏāḇâ*, and the "votive offering," *nêder*, which, we mentioned, God's people could of their own free will offer as sacrifices in the temple (Lev 23:37–38; Num 15:1–3; Ps 54:6): "For they gave according to their means, as I can testify, and beyond their means, of their own freewill" (2 Cor 8:3 RSV; see also 2 Cor 9:5). Indeed, it is by understanding Ananias and his wife's gift as a *nᵊḏāḇâ* they brought to the Christian assembly that one can account for their punishment when they chose to retain some of it (Acts 5:1–6). Unless redeemed as stipulated, a *nᵊḏāḇâ* could not be recalled because it ceased to be the worshipper's and became God's. We should also point out here the giving of believers in Philippi was viewed as an offering to God: "having received from Ephroditus the gifts you sent, a fragrant offering, a sacrifice acceptable and pleasing to God" (Phil 4:18 RSV).

Even prayers in the gathering of Christians were looked upon and understood in sacrificial terms. In Hebrews, for example, the writer encouraged his audience by use of sacrificial terminology to offer praises to God: "let us continually offer a sacrifice of praise to God, that is, the fruit of lips that confess his name" (Heb 13:15). In Revelation, as earlier noted, the collective prayers of God's people were visualized as incense rising from a burnt offering up to God (Rev 5:8).

We should point out here that the Lord's Supper, the activity in Christian assemblies (Acts 20:7; 1 Cor 11:20–33) with no parallel in temple activities, was seen too to mirror temple activities of sacrifice. This was so because it was viewed as a meal through which the sacrificial death of Jesus was either recalled or re-enacted making it, in some mysterious ways, his body and blood. This sacrificial significance of the meal accounts for Paul's warning to the church in Corinth, relative to pagan sacrifices, that their drinking from the cup and breaking of the bread was "a sharing," *koinōnia* (1 Cor 10:16), of the Lord's blood and body. He also warned them that they could not partake of the table of the Lord (*trapegsēs kuriou*) which was in their assemblies and the table of demons (*trapegsēs daimonion*) in pagan temples and shrines (1 Cor 10:21). Moreover, only if the Last Supper was taken in some sense as a sacrificial meal can we account for Paul's warning to the same church about erroneous beliefs some of them were falling prey to concerning the power of sacrificial foods.

> "Food will not bring us close to God." We are no worse off if we do not eat, and no better off if we do. (1 Cor 8:8)

> Do not be carried away by all kinds of strange teachings; for it is well for the heart to be strengthened by grace, not by regulations about food, which have not benefited those who observe them. (Heb 13:9)

Activities of Christian gatherings were therefore perceived as substitutes of temple activities, making the places where they gathered temple-like, and those who led them priestly. Since, as we showed earlier, temple activities constituted worship, activities in Christian assemblies were, like them, worship. We will therefore show in what follows, that preachers and teachers, prophets, and *presbuteroi-episkopoi* led the activities of Christian gatherings which made them, like priests, facilitators of worship which was a priestly task of their pastoral ministry.

Apostles and their counterparts as the facilitators of worship in Christian gatherings

In our discussion of preaching and teaching as the primary activities of pastoral ministry, we noted how apostolic and non-apostolic persons who undertook these shepherding responsibilities – the pastors in the New Testament – were variously designated as preachers and teachers, prophets, and *presbuteroi-episkopoi*. These figures were therefore church leaders precisely as referred to in 1 Thessalonians 5:12 and Hebrews 13:7 as *proistemenoi* and *hegoumenoi* respectively. For this reason, the churches which they led were admonished to give them respect (1 Cor 16:10; 1 Thess 5:12; 1 Tim 5:17) and to submit to them (Heb 13:17). Churches were also required to give respect to, and obey, those who were referred to as "labourers," *kopion*, and "fellow workers," *synergos* (1 Thess 5:12 and 1 Cor 16:16). Labourers (Rom 16:12; 1 Thess 5:12) and fellow workers (1 Cor 16:16; Rom 16:3; Phil 2:25; Col 4:7, 11; Phlm 1:1) were references, as Button and Rensburg's study demonstrated,[20] to these pastors as well. Consequently, to no one else other than their pastors were the churches instructed to submit or obey.

It was primarily by means of preaching and teaching in Christian gatherings that pastors exercised their leadership. (In fact, it is against the background of their teaching and preaching that the instructions to submit to, and obey them, make the most sense.) It would therefore have been unnatural for anyone else to be in charge of the activities in the gatherings when these pastors were present. This conclusion is very clear in the preaching and teaching activity of Christian gatherings because of the overwhelming evidence from the New Testament that it was the pastors who were responsible for them.

The conclusion above is confirmed by Alikin's study[21] which shows that *presbuteros*, one of the designations of these pastors in the New Testament, was taken from the Greek world where it was used to refer to persons responsible for meetings. Such persons watched over and kept order "in the community's meals and gatherings."[22] In other words, they were the ones who chaired meetings of their associations or religious meetings which were common.[23] The borrowing of this term and using it to denote these pastors in the Greco-Roman world must have been because they were the ones who were in charge of the activities of Christian gatherings.

We pointed out that in using temple terminology for activities of Christian gatherings, the apostles applied to themselves (and their non-apostolic counterparts) as the leaders of the Christian gatherings the designated roles of priests in the temple. This conclusion is clear when we consider Paul's words to the church in Corinth in a passage on giving and his rights to receive it, where he

---

20. Bruce Button and Fika J. Van Rensburg, "The 'House Churches' in Corinth," *Neot* 37, no. 1 (2003): 18–20.

21. Valeriy A. Alikin, *The Earliest History of Christian Gathering: Origin, Development and Content of the Christians Gathering in the First to Third Centuries* (Leiden: Brill, 2010), 71.

22. Alikin, *The Earliest History of Christian Gathering*, 71.

23. For more and the impact of these associations on Christian gatherings see Richard S. Ascough, *Early Christ Groups and Greco-Roman Associations: Organizational Models and Social Practices* (Eugene: Cascade Books, 2022).

likened preachers to priests (1 Cor 9:1–16). It was in view of his priestly task (of preaching and teaching the word in their gatherings) that Paul told them that he had the right to receive their gifts in the same way a priest who served God's people in the temple had the right to sharing their slain sacrifices and in their offerings:

> Do you know that those who are employed in the temple service get their food from the temple, and those who serve at the altar share in what is sacrificed at the altar? In the same way, the Lord commanded that those who proclaim the gospel should get their living by the gospel. (1 Cor 9:13–14)

This likening of preachers and teachers to priests is also hinted at in Paul's instructions to the Galatians. Just as the Israelites shared their sacrifices with their priests who served them in the temple, Paul instructed them to share with their teachers who preached and taught them in their gatherings for they too were carrying out a priestly task: "Those who are taught the word of God must share in all good things with their teacher" (Gal 6:6; see also 1 Tim 5:17–18).

But there is more. We mentioned that priests would bless God's people who came to the temple (Num 6:22–27; Deut 10:8; 21:5; see also Lev 9:22). The blessing of God's people was a responsibility they had been given by YHWH:

> The LORD spoke to Moses, saying: Speak to Aaron and his sons, saying, Thus you shall bless the Israelites: You shall say to them,
>
>> The LORD bless you and keep you;
>>> the LORD make his face to shine upon you, and be
>>>> gracious to you;
>>> the LORD lift up his countenance upon you, and give you
>>>> peace.
>>>>> So you shall put my name on the Israelites, and I will
>>>>>> bless them. (Num 6:22–27)

The blessing had four main elements: protection, radiance, grace, and peace. In time, as Fishbane's study demonstrates,[24] the priestly blessing would be reformulated, into shorter forms that touched on one or several of its elements. Psalm 67:1 epitomizes such reformulations where we have a shorter version of the blessing containing only the elements of grace and radiance found in the blessing:

---

24. Michael Fishbane, "Form and Reformulation of the Biblical Priestly Blessing," *JAOS* 103, no. 1 (1983): 115–121.

> May God be gracious to us and bless us
> > and make his face to shine upon us. (Ps 67:1; see also Pss 122:8; 128:5–6)

Shorter versions of the priestly blessing are also evident in the prayers which were inspired by it whereby an element of the blessing was the focus of a supplication – for grace (Pss 25:16; 119:29), for radiance (e.g. Pss 25:6; 80:3, 7), for peace (Pss 29:11; 125:5). Evidence of longer versions were there as well (Ps 4). In the first century, Jews would have been accustomed to various forms of the priestly blessing since it was a "synagogal act,"[25] being given in the synagogues as attested in the Mishna.[26] What all this displays is that in fulfilment of their shepherding responsibility to bless God's people, priests pronounced the blessing containing one, or a combination of, or all, of the elements in the blessing. In this respect, although we did not discuss when looking at Jesus's priestly tasks, we ought to view Jesus's words of peace, "peace be with you" (Luke 24:36; John 20:19), as a priestly blessing which contained only one of the blessing elements.

Since what we find in the Epistles is a reflection of what the apostles taught and said in Christian assemblies, and since there is evidence in the Epistles that the apostles (and their non-apostolic counterparts) blessed God's people, they must have pronounced blessing to those in Christian assemblies. In all the Epistles (except 1 John) and Revelation, there is a priestly blessing at the beginning and/or the end with the element of peace (Rom 15:33; 1 Pet 5:14; 3 John 15), or grace (e.g., 1 Cor 16:23; Gal 6:18; Phil 4:23; 2 Thess 3:18; Heb 13:25), or both (e.g., Gal 1:3; Col 1:2; 1 Pet 1:2). The apostles and their counterparts gave the priestly blessing as a priestly task of their pastoral ministry because, in leading the activities of Christian assemblies, they likened their pastoral ministry to that of priests.

The apostles and their non-apostolic counterparts were, therefore, just as priests in the temple, facilitators of worship in Christian gatherings. By managing the activities of Christian gatherings, they were, according to the New Testament, undertaking the priestly task of their pastoral ministry. Following this New Testament perspective, it is incumbent on pastors to undertake diligently this priestly task of pastoral ministry when the members of the churches they are responsible for come together. In so doing, they facilitate the worship

---

25. P. A. H. de Boer, "Numbers IV 27," *VT* 32, no. 1 (1982): 3–13, 11.
26. See *Meg.* 4:6ff, *Sotah* 7:2, 6.

of God by his people which is the basic reason for which they assemble, and the prime activity which characterizes and defines them.

When pastors fail in their priestly task to facilitate worship, the potential of Christian gatherings becoming what the temple was designed for are compromised. They are less likely to be places for God's people to hear and learn from his word, to praise and thank him, to seek and find his forgiveness, and unburden themselves before him. There is also a high likelihood of Christian gatherings not being places where God's people step into the transcendental and spiritual dimensions with, therefore, the ever-present possibility of the in-breaking of his power and revelations amongst them, and the experience of his subliminal presence variously in, for example, visions, comfort, thirst for righteousness, wonder, release, joy, and peace.

6

Practical Recommendations for Primary Activities in Pastoral Ministry

Our whole-Bible study which is based on Jesus as the chief shepherd – which we have demonstrated is itself rooted in the shepherding responsibilities of prophets and priests in the Old Testament – has established that pastoral ministry is defined by three distinct activities: preaching and teaching God's word, caring for those in difficulties, and facilitating worship. Although it is tempting to discuss how that pastoral ministry can be carried out today, such a discussion is beyond the scope of this study. My primary concern has been to lay out the Bible's perspective on pastoral ministry in the hope that my readers will seek out pastoral ministry handbooks to help them conduct these activities, or to envision for themselves how they can be conducted in their contexts.

Nonetheless, with respect to current resources for the study of the Bible, I will conclude by offering some brief practical recommendations that can help pastors fulfil one aspect of pastoral ministry: the teaching and preaching of the word. I single it out as worthy of special attention in a study of this nature because, as we demonstrated, giving the word of God is the *primary activity* of pastoral ministry. I hope that the recommendations I advance here will help those training to be pastors, and pastors alike, who read this book have an idea of what they should strategically invest in and direct their energies towards in order to deliver today on this fundamental activity in biblically envisioned pastoral ministry.

The Bible's Double-Sided Reality

The Scriptures can be very simple and clear as the word of God whereby anyone or everyone who can read, including school-age children, can understand them, be enlightened by them, and obey their teachings. This clarity was manifest in my own African heritage when the Bible was translated into African languages. African Christians without any training or formal education did not need the missionaries to interpret the Bible for them. Once they heard the Scriptures in their languages, they understood them, and began applying them to their lives in ways the missionaries might never have anticipated.

However, the picture I have portrayed of the Bible's clarity can be, to a point, very deceptive given the historical, literary, complex, and voluminous nature of the Bible which makes the Scriptures at the same time quite difficult to make sense of and some of its content beyond the reach of one's interpretation. Consequently the Scriptures may not be clear to many, including those in clerical garb who are designated to preach and teach the Bible. For this reason, there are three prerequisites that I strongly want to suggest have to be met if pastors are to fulfil their pastoral ministry of giving God's word to God's people. They are all premised on the fact that the capacity of one to preach or teach anything adequately is hinged upon his/her mastery of the content of what is to be preached or taught. The communication principle that ignorance or scanty knowledge of content compromises its effective communication applies to the mastery of the Bible's contents and the ability to effectively preach and teach holy Scriptures. With this clear, I now turn to my recommendations.

Approaching the Bible as One Book

The books of the Bible are not a random collection to be read in isolation from each other, but rather are like a book, cohering and giving a story when read together in conjunction. Therefore, the first prerequisite for preaching and teaching the word is that a pastor must have a firm grasp of the overall message of the Scriptures. To be more precise, a pastor must be familiar with the main storyline of the Bible. S/he must clearly see and understand its plot, broadly conceived, from creation, human rebellion against God's rule ("the fall"), Abraham, Israel, David, to Christ, church, and the new creation. Even if not seen this way, at the very least a pastor must perceive the threads that run through the Bible's contents, the Old and New Testament, which then make it an integrated whole.

Understanding the overall message of the Bible naturally helps pastors actually preach the good news from God, for the Bible's main message is captured in its metanarrative, which is about the salvation of humanity and the world. Pastors who understand the overall message of the Bible help God's people, through their preaching and teaching, to appreciate God's pre-eminent message to humanity, his concerns with the world, and his ultimate ends with it. Understanding the overall message of the Bible also help pastors to approach and interpret the individual Bible texts from the perspective of the whole Bible. Such Bible interpretations promote, if not ensure, the preaching and teaching of God's word in reality by mitigating pontifical, highly personalized, culturally trapped, fanciful, and wild readings of the Bible that compromise a pastor's ability to give God's word to his people, despite his or her preaching and teaching from the Bible.

Acquiring a firm grasp of the Bible's overall content requires diligent study. It requires one to take time reading and re-reading the Bible deliberately as one book, carefully retaining knowledge of what is read, in order to both follow the Scriptures' narrative and make connections between the contents of books, and/or texts, of the Bible. In so doing one eventually makes sense of the Bible's overall content. There are no alternatives to such rigorous readings of the Bible if one is to come to terms with its main storyline and cohesiveness. A pastor would be greatly aided and stimulated in such an exercise by turning to biblical theology books that seek to lay out overviews of the Bible and demonstrate Scriptures' cohesiveness.[1]

Understanding the Bible's Key Themes

Since the Bible addresses subjects of pressing, even perpetual, existential/theological concerns, the second prerequisite for teaching and preaching the word is that a pastor must be well versed with the major contours of the content of the Scriptures. These subjects constitute its key contents because they preoccupy its narratives. Furthermore, they are the ones mainly addressed in its propositional or direct messages, and dominate its epistolary and didactic literature. In this respect, I suggest four main subjects that stand out in the Bible's contents about which pastors must learn and understand from Scriptures, namely, "God and

---

1. Here are four good examples including my recent study: Nyende, *God's Dwelling and Kingdom*; Frank Thielman, *The New Creation and the Storyline of Scripture*, SSBT (Wheaton: Crossway, 2021); Craig G. Bartholomew and Michael W. Goheen, *The Drama of Scripture: Finding Our Place in the Biblical Story*, 2nd ed. (Grand Rapids: Baker Academic, 2014); and Thomas Schreiner, *The King in his Beauty: A Biblical Theology of the Old and New Testaments* (Grand Rapids: Baker Academic, 2013).

his nature," "his ways and those contrary to them," "his salvation," and "the identity, vocation and destiny of his people."

Knowledge of the Bible's contents on these subjects enables pastors to help God's people to increase in their knowledge of God and of his Son the Lord Jesus, understand and appreciate the ways they ought to live, and orientate them to what ought to be their primary identity and calling, and to their eternal hope. Such knowledge also helps pastors in their preaching and teaching to make connections between the Bible text that is the subject of their preaching or teaching and other similar texts in the Bible. Doing so feeds God's people his word – it fosters their knowledge of God's word, thus helping to engender their growth in Christ. It also demonstrates to God's flock that the Scriptures contain the word of God and should accordingly be heard and read, and subsequently embraced with faith for daily living and orientations to the seen and unseen world.

Biblical studies books that deal with God,[2] or salvation,[3] or God's ways,[4] or his people[5] and their destiny[6] are great resources which pastors can turn to for inquiry and learning to help them get a good grasp of what the Bible teaches about them.

---

2. See for example Ben Withering III and Laura M. Ice, *The Shadow of the Almighty: Father, Son, and Spirit in Biblical Perspective* (Grand Rapids: Eerdmans, 2002); Peter Toon, *Our Triune God: A Biblical Portrayal of the Trinity* (Wheaton: Bridgepoint, 1996); and J. I. Packer, *Knowing God* (Leicester: Inter-Varsity Press, 1993).

3. See for example Nicholas T. Wright, *The Day the Revolution Began: Reconsidering the Meaning of Jesus's Crucifixion* (New York: HarperOne, 2016); Christopher J. H. Wright, *Salvation Belongs to Our God: Celebrating the Bible's Central Story*, Christian Doctrine in Global Perspective (Downers Grove: IVP Academic, 2008); Willem Vangemeren, *The Progress of Redemption: The Story of Salvation from Creation to the New Jerusalem* (Grand Rapids: Baker Books, 1998).

4. See for example Richard A. Burridge, *Imitating Jesus: An Inclusive Approach to New Testament Ethics* (Grand Rapids: Eerdmans, 2007); John Muillenburg, *The Way of Israel: Biblical Faith and Ethics* (New York: HarperCollins, 1979); and Rudolf Schnackenburg, *The Moral Teaching Of The New Testament* (Freiburg: Herder, 1965).

5. See for example Benjamin L. Gladd, *From Adam and Israel to the Church: A Biblical Theology of the People of God*, ESBT (Downers Grove: IVP Academic, 2019); Brian S. Rosner, *Known by God: A Biblical Theology of Personal Identity*, Biblical Theology for Life (Grand Rapids: Zondervan Academic, 2017); Jo Bailey Wells, *God's Holy People: A Theme in Biblical Theology*, JSOTsup, vol. 305 (Sheffield: Sheffield Academic Press, 2000).

6. See for example J. Richard Middleton, *A New Heaven and a New Earth: Reclaiming Biblical Eschatology* (Grand Rapids: Baker Academic, 2014); Mitchell L. Chase, *Resurrection Hope and the Death of Death*, SSBT (Wheaton: Crossway, 2022); Richard Bauckham, *Bible and Mission: Christian Witness in a Postmodern World* (Grand Rapids: Baker Academic, 2012).

Necessary Background and Literary Knowledge for Reading the Bible

The third prerequisite for teaching and preaching the word are specific knowledge and skills that help to explore, probe, and ultimately make sense of any biblical text that is the subject of preaching or teaching. Complex Bible contents and genre, and particularly the ones far removed from one's own experiences, mores, common knowledge, and literary sensibilities, require possession of certain knowledge to unlock. Such knowledge includes the geographical, religio-cultural, philosophical, political, and socio-economic knowledge pertaining to Israel and that of its neighbours. Knowledge that is required also includes that of the Greco-Roman world, characteristics of those biblical literary genres that are unlike our own, and a rudimentary reading competency of Hebrew and Greek – having a basic Hebrew and Greek vocabulary and able to identify the forms of their words.[7]

Skills required include how to interpret Scriptures in the light of their general and specific historical contexts as well as in the light of the rest of the Bible. Alongside this skill, and not mutually exclusive from it, is the interpretation of texts of the Bible in the light of the literary genres they belong to. Lastly, skills are required on how to apply the historical message of the Scriptures once established – the application of the message of those Scriptures as was most likely understood by the initial recipients of the message to contemporary times, is necessary.

Such knowledge and skills are acquired through appropriate teaching and exposure. The following critical resources are considerably helpful, if not indispensable, in attaining the knowledge and/or skills alluded to. There are books that help readers with the know-how of making sense of the Bible in ways faithful to the revelatory, historical, and literary nature of Scriptures.[8] There are also books that discuss the world of the Bible – from the Ancient

---

7. Such enables the pastor to engage the original language in the interpretation of a Bible text or texts. For more on this, see Carl E. Sanders II, "Biblical Language Instruction by the Book: Rethinking the *Status Quaestionis*," *Teach Theology and Religion* 20 (2017): 216–229. http://doi:org/10:1111/teth:12390.

8. Some good examples of resources for Bible interpretation are: Nicholas G. Piotrowski, *In All the Scriptures: The Three Contexts of Biblical Hermeneutics*, with a foreword by Graeme Goldsworthy (Downers Grove: IVP Academic, 2021); Gordon D. Fee and Douglas Stuart, *How to Read the Bible for All Its Worth*, 4th ed. (Grand Rapids: Zondervan, 2014); and R. C. Sproul, *Knowing Scripture* (Downers Grove: InterVarsity Press 1977).

Near East,[9] to the Greco-Roman World.[10] Then there are Bible commentaries which provide knowledge of the world of the Bible and use it to enlighten the message of a book of the Bible through their verse-by-verse commentary from the first to the last chapter of the given book. But Bible commentaries are not all of the same depth or purpose. There are on the one end of the spectrum highly technical, specialized Bible commentaries which comment primarily on the original text, assuming that the reader has knowledge of the original languages of the Bible,[11] while on the other end are Bible commentaries that are more concrete and relatively simple to follow. The latter also normally relate their historical and philological insights of the Bible book's content to the present world and concerns of believers today.[12] Other commentaries are a mixture, more or less, of these two kinds of Bible commentaries.[13]

Bible dictionaries assist readers with encyclopedic religio-cultural, philosophical, socio-economic and political knowledge through an alphabetically arranged entry of biblical books, customs, events, ideas, places, technical terms and so forth. They are therefore very useful to pastors in offering them introductory and, therefore, quick general knowledge related to the book, texts, or text they are studying. Like Bible dictionaries, study Bibles also offer introductory and quick contextual knowledge concerning the Bible. However, unlike Bible dictionaries, the information is structured sequentially on the order of the books of the Bible from Genesis to Revelation. Accordingly, for every book of the Bible, they first offer an introduction and an overview of its content. They then follow this by giving the text of the Bible book in whole (in the given Bible

---

9. See, for example, Don C. Benjamin and Victor H. Matthews, *Social World of Ancient Israel: 1250–587 BCE* (Grand Rapids: Baker Academic, 2005); John S. Greer, John W. Hilber, and John H. Walton, eds., *Behind the Scenes of the Old Testament: Cultural, Social and Historical Contexts* (Grand Rapids: Baker Academic, 2018); and John H. Walton, *Ancient Near Eastern Thought and the Old Testament: Introducing the Conceptual World of the Hebrew Bible* (Grand Rapids: Baker Academic, 2018).

10. See, for example, Everett Ferguson, *Backgrounds of Early Christianity*, 3rd ed. (Grand Rapids: Eerdmans, 2003); Mark A. Chauncy, *Greco-Roman Culture and the Galilee of Jesus*, SNTSMS 134 (Cambridge: Cambridge University Press, 2005); and Craig Keener and John H. Walton, eds., *NIV Cultural Backgrounds Study Bible: Bringing to Life the Ancient World of Scripture* (Grand Rapids: Zondervan, 2016).

11. Represented in the following Bible commentary series: Hermeneia, NICOT, NICNT, NIGTC, and Word Biblical Commentaries.

12. See, for example NIV Application series commentaries, New Interpreter's Bible commentaries, The Bible Speaks Today commentary series and Expositor's Bible commentaries.

13. See, for example, Baker Exegetical Commentaries, Pillar New Testament Commentaries, Sacra Pagina commentaries, and Zondervan Exegetical Commentaries.

version) together with cross-references on the margins. Finally, verse-by-verse commentary on that book is given in the footnotes.

Hebrew and Greek lexicons give meaning of words in the original languages. Books on the meaning of Old and/or New Testament words complement lexicons by providing easily accessible information on Hebrew or Greek Bible words for a better understanding of a Bible text.[14] Interlinear translations complement lexicons and Bible word books because they help readers see how the original is conveyed into contemporary language whilst also alerting them to words whose meaning may need to be further explored in a lexicon or Bible word books for better understanding of the text.

A pastor ought therefore to consult these critical resources more or less regularly in the course of making clear sense of a Bible text in order to preach or teach it. S/he also needs to seek out avenues through which s/he can be tutored or exposed to the knowledge and skills alluded to, by biblical scholars who have the requisite knowledge and skills.

Having the required knowledge and skills ensure that it is the Scriptures (their meaning and application) that are actually the subject of preaching and teaching. Where this is present, pastors are able to preach and teach indeed the word of God whether it is based on lectionary readings, or readings selected for a given day, or readings based on seasons set in the liturgical calendar of the church. Having the required knowledge and skills to interpret texts of the Bible also enables pastors to pick an appropriate Bible text or texts to address a topic of present concern, or address a topic dictated upon them by specific situations or occasions.

Conclusion

To sum up my recommendations: a grasp of the Bible's main message, familiarity with its key subjects, and biblical historico-literary knowledge together with skills in Bible interpretation, are conditions that pastors today should aspire to meet. When they meet these conditions, pastors are truly and competently able to preach the word of God to their flock, and to faithfully pass on to them its teachings.

---

14. See, for example, William D. Mounce, *Mounce's Complete Expository Dictionary of Old and New Testament Words* (Grand Rapids: Zondervan Academic, 2009); Harvest House Publishers, *The Harvest Handbook of Key Bible Words New Testament: Understand Their Original Meanings and Apply Them to Your Life* (Harvest House Publishers, 2018); and Mark L. Strauss and Tremper Longman III, *The Baker Expository Dictionary of Biblical Words* (Grand Rapids: Baker Academic, 2023).

Bibliography

Abbott-Smith, G. *A Manual Greek Lexicon*. Edinburgh: T&T Clark, 1999.

Akin, Daniel L. *Pastoral Theology: Theological Foundations for Who a Pastor is and What he Does*. Nashville: B&H Academic, 2017.

Alikin, Valeriy A. *The Earliest History of Christian Gathering: Origin, Development and Content of the Christians Gathering in the First to Third Centuries*. Leiden: Brill, 2010.

Ascough, Richard S. *Early Christ Groups and Greco-Roman Associations: Organizational Models and Social Practices*. Eugene: Cascade Books, 2022.

Attridge, Harold W. "How Priestly Is the 'High Priestly Prayer' of John 17?" *CBQ* 75, no. 1 (2013): 1–14.

Aune, David E. *Revelation 1–5*. WBC 52A. Nashville: Thomas Nelson, 1997.

Baltzer, Klaus. *Deutero-Isaiah: A Commentary on Isaiah 40–55*. Hermeneia. Philadelphia: Fortress Press, 2001.

Bartholomew, Craig G. and Michael W. Goheen. *The Drama of Scripture: Finding Our Place in the Biblical Story*. 2nd edition. Grand Rapids: Baker Academic, 2014.

Bauckham, Richard. *Bible and Mission: Christian Witness in a Postmodern World*. Grand Rapids: Baker Academic, 2012.

Benjamin, Don C. and Victor H. Matthews. *Social World of Ancient Israel: 1250–587 BCE*. Grand Rapids: Baker Academic, 2005.

Berinyuu, Abraham Adu. *Towards Theory and Practice of Pastoral Counseling in Africa*. Bern: Peter Lang, 1990.

Block, Daniel I. *The Book of Ezekiel Chapters 25–48*. NICOT. Grand Rapids: Eerdmans, 1998.

Bridge, Edward J. "Loyalty, Dependency and Status with YHWH: The Use of *'bd* in the Psalms." *VT* 59 (2009): 360–378.

Brown, Raymond E. *The Gospel according to John XIII–XXI*. Vol 29A, AB. Garden City: Doubleday & Co., 1970.

Burke, Trevor J., Andrew S. Malone, and Brian S. Rosner, eds., *Paul as Pastor*. London: T&T Clark, 2018.

Burridge, Richard A. *Imitating Jesus: An Inclusive Approach to New Testament Ethics*. Grand Rapids: Eerdmans, 2007.

Button, Bruce and Fika J. Van Rensburg. "The 'House Churches' in Corinth." *Neot* 37, no. 1 (2003): 1–28.

Carson, D. A. "Do the Work of an Evangelist." *Them* 39, no. 1 (2014): 1–4.

Chase, Mitchell L. *Resurrection Hope and the Death of Death*. SSBT. Wheaton: Crossway, 2022.

Chauncy, Mark A. *Greco-Roman Culture and the Galilee of Jesus*. SNTSMS 134. Cambridge: Cambridge University Press, 2005.

Collins, John. "A Monocultural Usage: διακον-words in Classical, Hellenistic, and Patristic Sources." *VigChr* 66 (2012): 290–295.

Croft, Brian. *The Pastor's Ministry: Biblical Priorities for Faithful Shepherds*. Grand Rapids: Zondervan, 2015.

Croy, N. C. *The Mutilation of Mark's Gospel*. Nashville: Abingdon Press, 2003.

de Boer, P. A. H. "Numbers IV 27." *VT* 32, no. 1 (1982): 3–13.

de Roest, Henk. *Collaborative Practical Theology: Engaging Practitioners in Research on Christian Practices*. Leiden: Brill, 2020.

Eberhart, Christian A. "A Neglected Feature of Sacrifice in the Hebrew Bible: Remarks on the Burning Rite on the Altar." *HTR* 97, no. 4 (2004): 485–493.

Edwards, William R. "Participants in What we Proclaim: Recovering Paul's Narrative of Pastoral Ministry." *Them* 39, no. 3 (2014): 455–469.

Fee, Gordon D. and Douglas Stuart. *How to Read the Bible for All Its Worth*. 4th edition. Grand Rapids: Zondervan, 2014.

Ferguson, Everett. *Backgrounds of Early Christianity*. 3rd edition. Grand Rapids: Eerdmans, 2003.

Feuillet, Andre. *The Priesthood of Christ and His Ministers*. Translated into English by Matthew J. O'Connell. Garden City: Doubleday, 1975.

Filson, Floyd V. "The Christian Teacher in the First Century." *JBL* 60.3 (1941): 317–328.

Fishbane, Michael. "Form and Reformulation of the Biblical Priestly Blessing." *JAOSy* 103, no. 1 (1983): 115–121.

Fitzmyer, Joseph A. "The Structured Ministry of the Church in the Pastoral Epistles." *CBQ* 66, no. 4 (2004): 582–596.

France, R. T. *The Gospel of Matthew*. NICNT. Grand Rapids: Eerdmans, 2007.

Gilmour, S. Maclean. "'Pastoral Care' in the New Testament Church." *NTS* 10 (1964): 393–398.

Gladd, Benjamin L. *From Adam and Israel to the Church: A Biblical Theology of the People of God*. ESBT. Downers Grove: IVP Academic, 2019.

Graham, Elaine L. *Transforming Practise: Pastoral Theology in an Age of Uncertainty*. London: Mowbray, 1996.

Greer, John S., John W. Hilber, and John H. Walton, eds. *Behind the Scenes of the Old Testament: Cultural, Social and Historical Contexts*. Grand Rapids: Baker Academic, 2018.

Grothe, Jonathan F. *Reclaiming Patterns of Pastoral Ministry: Jesus and Paul*. St. Louise: Concordia, 1988.

Hartin, Patrick J. "Disciples as authorities within Matthew's Christians-Jewish community." *Neotestamentica* 32, no. 2 (1998): 389–404.

Harvest House Publishers. *The Harvest Handbook of Key Bible Words New Testament: Understand Their Original Meanings and Apply Them to Your Life*. Harvest House Publishers, 2018.

Heil, John Paul. "Jesus as the Unique High Priest in the Gospel of John." *CBQ* 57, no. 4 (1995): 730.

Hess, Richard S. *Israelite Religions: An Archaeological and Biblical Survey.* Grand Rapids: Baker Academics, 2007.

Holladay, William L. *Jeremiah 1: A Commentary on the Book of the Prophet Jeremiah Chapters 1 – 25.* Hermenia. Philadelphia: Fortress Press, 1986.

Hoyle, David. *The Pattern of our Calling: Ministry Yesterday, Today and Tomorrow.* London: SCM Press, 2016.

Hughes, R. Kent. *The Pastor's Book: A Comprehensive and Practical Guide to Pastoral Ministry.* Wheaton: Crossway, 2015.

Johnson, Paul E. "A Theology of Pastoral Care." *JOHR* 3, no. 2 (1964): 171–175.

Keener, Craig S. *Miracles Today: The Supernatural Work of God in the Modern World.* Grand Rapids: Baker Academics, 2021.

Keener, Craig and John H. Walton, eds. *NIV Cultural Backgrounds Study Bible: Bringing to Life the Ancient World of Scripture.* Grand Rapids: Zondervan, 2016.

Kintoi, Hannah W. and Douglas W. Waruta, eds. *Pastoral Care in African Christianity: Challenging Essays in Pastoral Theology.* 2nd edition. Nairobi: Acton Publishers, 2000.

Kittel, Gerhard, ed. *Theologisches Wörterbuch zum Neun Testament.* Stuttgart: W. Kohlhammer, 1935.

Korpel, Marjo C. A. "Metaphors in Isaiah LV." *VT* 46, no. 1 (1996): 49–50.

Köstenberger, Andreas J. *A Theology of John's Gospel and Letters: The Word of Christ, the Son of God.* Grand Rapids: Zondervan, 2015.

Laniak, Timothy S. *Shepherds after My Own Heart: Pastoral Traditions and Leadership in the Bible.* NSBT 20. Downers Grove: InterVarsity Press 2006.

Lartey, Emmanuel Y. *In Living Colour: An Intercultural Approach to Pastoral Care and Counselling.* London: SPCK, 1997.

Lee, Dorothy A. "'Signs and works': The Miracles in the Gospels of Mark and John." *Colloq* 47, no. 1 (2015): 89–101.

Leeb, Carolyn S. "The Widows in the Hebrew Bible: Homeless and Post-menopausal." *Proceedings* 21 (2001): 61–67.

Liefeld, Walter L. *Ephesians.* IVPNTC. Downers Grove: InterVarsity Press 1997.

Lincoln, Andrew T. *Ephesians.* Word Biblical Commentary 42. Dallas: Word Publishers, 1990.

Lindsay, Dennis R. "What is Truth? Ἀλήθεια in the Gospel of John." *ResQ* 35, no. 3 (1993): 129–145.

Magezi, Vhumani. "Practical Theology in Africa: Situation, Approaches, Framework and Agenda Proposition." *IJPT* 23, no. 1 (2019): 115–135.

Malherbe, Abraham J. *Paul and the Thessalonians: The Philosophic Tradition of Pastoral Care.* Eugene: Wipf and Stock, 2011.

———. "'Pastoral Care' in the Thessalonian Church." *NTS* 36 (1990): 375–391.

Marcus, Joel. "Passover and Last Supper Revisited." *NTS* 59, no. 4 (2013): 303–324.

Masson, R. "Analogy and Metaphoric Process." *TS* 62 (2001): 571–596.

Mavis, W. C. "Jesus's Influence on the Pastoral Ministry." *Theology Today* 4, no. 3 (1947): 357–367.

McKenzie, John L. "The Word of God in the Old Testament." *TS* 21 (1960): 183–206.

Middleton, J. Richard. *A New Heaven and a New Earth: Reclaiming Biblical Eschatology*. Grand Rapids: Baker Academic, 2014.

Mounce, William D. *Complete Expository Dictionary of Old and New Testament Words*. Grand Rapids: Zondervan Academic, 2009.

Muillenburg, John. *The Way of Israel: Biblical Faith and Ethics*. New York: HarperCollins, 1979.

Nwachuku, Daisy and Jean Masamba ma Mpolo, eds. *Pastoral Care and Counselling in Africa Today*. African Pastoral Studies vol. 1. Bern: Peter Lang, 1991.

Nyende, Peter. *God's Dwelling and Kingdom: A Christian Biblical Theology*. Carlisle: Langham Global Library, 2023.

Oden, Thomas. *Pastoral Theology*. San Francisco: Harper and Row, 1983.

Packer, J. I. *Knowing God*. Leicester: Inter-Varsity Press, 1993.

Padilla, Osvaldo. *The Acts of the Apostles: Interpretation, History and Theology*. London: Apollos, 2016.

Pao, David W. "Waiters as Preachers: Acts 6:1–7 and the Lucan Table Fellowship Motif." *JBL* 130, no. 1 (2011): 127–144.

Piotrowski, Nicholas G. *In All the Scriptures: The Three Contexts of Biblical Hermeneutics*. Foreword by Graeme Goldsworthy. Downers Grove: IVP Academic, 2021.

Reed, Carson E. "Practical Theology in Diverse Ethnic Community: Matthew's Gospel as a Model of Ministry." *ResQ* 60, no. 3 (2018): 163–170.

Rosner, Brian S. *Known by God: A Biblical Theology of Personal Identity*. Biblical Theology for Life. Grand Rapids: Zondervan Academic, 2017.

Ross, Allen P. *Biblical Worship from the Garden to the New Creation: Recalling the Hope of Glory*. Grand Rapids: Kregel Academic and Professional, 2006.

Sanders II, Carl E. "Biblical Language Instruction by the Book: Rethinking the *Status Quaestionis*." *Teach Theology and Religion*, 20 (2017): 216–229. http:/doi:org/10:1111/teth:12390.

Schnackenburg, Rudolf. *The Moral Teaching of The New Testament*. Freiburg: Herder, 1965.

Scholer, J. M. *Proleptic Priests: Priesthood in the Epistle to the Hebrews*. JSNTSup 49. Sheffield: JSOT Press, 1991.

Schreiner, Thomas. *The King in his Beauty: A Biblical Theology of the Old and New Testaments*. Grand Rapids: Baker Academic, 2013.

Snaith, Norman H. "Sacrifices in the Old Testament." *VT* 7, no. 3 (1957): 308–317.

Spencer, F. Scott. "Neglected Widows in Acts 6:1–7." *CBQ* 56, no. 4 (1994): 715–733.

Sproul, R. C. *Knowing Scripture*. Downers Grove: InterVarsity Press 1977.

Stott, John R. W. "Ideals of Pastoral Ministry." *Bsac* 146, no. 581 (1989): 3–11.

Strauss, Mark L. and Tremper Longman III. *The Baker Expository Dictionary of Biblical Words*. Grand Rapids: Baker Academic, 2023.

Sukenik, E. E. *Ancient Synagogues in Palestine and Greece*. London: Oxford University Press, 1934.

Swetnam, James. "ὁ ἀπόστολος in Hebrews 3:1." *Biblica* 89, no. 2 (2008): 255–259.

Thielman, Frank. *The New Creation and the Storyline of Scripture*. SSBT. Wheaton: Crossway, 2021.

Thompson, James W. *Pastoral Ministry According to Paul: A Biblical Vision*. Grand Rapids: Eerdmans, 2006.

Toon, Peter. *Our Triune God: A Biblical Portrayal of the Trinity*. Wheaton: Bridgepoint, 1996.

Vangemeren, Willem. *The Progress of Redemption: The Story of Salvation from Creation to the New Jerusalem*. Grand Rapids: Baker Books, 1998.

Walton, John H. *Ancient Near Eastern Thought and the Old Testament: Introducing the Conceptual World of the Hebrew Bible*. Grand Rapids: Baker Academic, 2018.

Wells, Jo Bailey. *God's Holy People: A Theme in Biblical Theology*. JSOTSup, vol. 305. Sheffield: Sheffield Academic Press, 2000.

Willimon, William H. *Pastor: A Reader for Ordained Ministry*. Nashville: Abingdon Press, 2002.

Withering III, Ben and Laura M. Ice. *The Shadow of the Almighty: Father, Son, and Spirit in Biblical Perspective*. Grand Rapids: Eerdmans, 2002.

Wright, Christopher J. H. *Salvation Belongs to Our God: Celebrating the Bible's Central Story*. Christian Doctrine in Global Perspective. Downers Grove: IVP Academic, 2008.

Wright, Nicholas T. *The Day the Revolution Began: Reconsidering the Meaning of Jesus's Crucifixion*. New York: HarperOne, 2016.

Index

A
apostles
  and care for people through miracles 81, 83, 85
  and word of blessing 115
  care for the poor 89–91
  care for widows 88
  comforting God's people by giving God's timely word 72
  commissioned by Jesus 10, 35, 48, 60
  preachers/teachers of God's word 47, 49–50, 52, 55, 57, 60, 63
  priestly tasks 100, 108, 112–13, 115
  prophets 50, 52

C
comfort
  and *parakaleō* 73
  as binding the brokenhearted 23–24, 29–30
  as care 85, 87
  through God's timely word 30

E
elders-bishops (*presbuteroi-episkopoi*) 50, 52, 56, 58, 84
  and care for people through miracles 84
  apostles 52
  appointing of 54
  comforting God's people by giving God's timely word 73
  preachers/teachers of God's word 55–56
  priestly tasks 112
  Timothy 55
  Titus 55
evangelists
  elders-bishops (*presbuteroi-episkopoi*) 56
  Philip 56
  preachers of good news 57
  preachers/teachers of God's word 56
  Timothy 57
  Timothy and the work of 57

J
Jesus
  and care for God's people through miracles 79, 81
  chief shepherd 10, 32–33, 39, 61, 117
  comforting God's people through God's timely word 72
  pastoral ministry 11
  priest 37–38, 100–2, 105, 115
  prophet 35–36, 79
  rabbi/teacher of God's word 45–47

M
metaphors
  binding wounded sheep as binding/healing the brokenhearted 22–24, 29
  God's word as food 18, 68
  God's word as pasture 17
  sheep as God's people 15–16
  shepherds as leaders of God's people 15, 25, 31
  shepherd-teachers/shepherds and teachers 59–61
  wandering astray as disobedience 21

P
preacher/teachers. *See also* apostles, elders-bishops, evangelists
  Barnabas 53
  James 56
  Lucius 53
  Niger 53
  Simeon 53

priests
  and offering of sacrifices 94
  givers of blessings 97–98, 114–15
  givers of the word 25, 97
  servants in God's house 93
  shepherds 25, 27
prophets. *See* also Jesus
  Agabus 51
  Barnabas 53
  binding the brokenhearted 29–31, 71
  comforting God's people through miracles 31, 72
  givers of God's timely word 29–30, 51, 53, 72
  givers of the word 25–26
  in Jerusalem 53
  Paul 50, 52
  Silas 53

S

sacrifices. *See* also priests
  burnt offering 94–96, 99, 111
  free-will offering 96, 111
  grain offering 96
  peace offering 96, 108
  proserxesthai/proskunein 101, 106
  sin offering 95, 102–5
  votive offering 96, 111
shepherds. *See* also elders-bishops, Jesus, priests, prophets
  executive and non-executive roles of 11, 33, 39
  leaders. *See* metaphors
  poimēn/poimenas 11, 61
  ra'ah 13

W

word of God
  as food. *See* metaphors
  as good news 64
  as pasture. *See* metaphors
  content of preaching/teaching 63
  dabar 40
  for faith 64
  for growth 67
  logos 39–40, 47, 110
  timely 30, 51, 72

Langham Literature and its imprints are a ministry of Langham Partnership.

Langham Partnership is a global fellowship working in pursuit of the vision God entrusted to its founder John Stott –

> *to facilitate the growth of the church in maturity and Christ-likeness through raising the standards of biblical preaching and teaching.*

Our vision is to see churches in the Majority World equipped for mission and growing to maturity in Christ through the ministry of pastors and leaders who believe, teach and live by the word of God.

Our mission is to strengthen the ministry of the word of God through:
- nurturing national movements for biblical preaching
- fostering the creation and distribution of evangelical literature
- enhancing evangelical theological education

especially in countries where churches are under-resourced.

Our ministry

Langham Preaching partners with national leaders to nurture indigenous biblical preaching movements for pastors and lay preachers all around the world. With the support of a team of trainers from many countries, a multi-level programme of seminars provides practical training, and is followed by a programme for training local facilitators. Local preachers' groups and national and regional networks ensure continuity and ongoing development, seeking to build vigorous movements committed to Bible exposition.

Langham Literature provides Majority World preachers, scholars and seminary libraries with evangelical books and electronic resources through publishing and distribution, grants and discounts. The programme also fosters the creation of indigenous evangelical books in many languages, through writer's grants, strengthening local evangelical publishing houses, and investment in major regional literature projects, such as one volume Bible commentaries like *The Africa Bible Commentary* and *The South Asia Bible Commentary*.

Langham Scholars provides financial support for evangelical doctoral students from the Majority World so that, when they return home, they may train pastors and other Christian leaders with sound, biblical and theological teaching. This programme equips those who equip others. Langham Scholars also works in partnership with Majority World seminaries in strengthening evangelical theological education. A growing number of Langham Scholars study in high quality doctoral programmes in the Majority World itself. As well as teaching the next generation of pastors, graduated Langham Scholars exercise significant influence through their writing and leadership.

To learn more about Langham Partnership and the work we do visit **langham.org**

www.ingramcontent.com/pod-product-compliance
Lightning Source LLC
Chambersburg PA
CBHW070541170426
43200CB00011B/2500